Canadian
CONFEDERATE CRUISER

The Story of the Steamer Queen Victoria

JOHN G. LANGLEY
award-winning author of *Steam Lion*

NIMBUS
PUBLISHING
— NIMBUS.CA —

Copyright © 2018, John G. Langley

All rights reserved. No part of this book may be reproduced, stored in a retrieval system or transmitted in any form or by any means without the prior written permission from the publisher, or, in the case of photocopying or other reprographic copying, permission from Access Copyright, 1 Yonge Street, Suite 1900, Toronto, Ontario M5E 1E5.

Nimbus Publishing Limited
3660 Strawberry Hill Street, Halifax, NS, B3K 5A9
(902) 455-4286 nimbus.ca

NB1363

Cover and interior design: Andrew Herygers
Editor: Paula Sarson
Cover image: Oil painting of *Napoleon III*, sister ship (and identical in all respects) to *Queen Victoria*, courtesy of the Confederation Centre.

Library and Archives Canada Cataloguing in Publication

    Langley, John G., author
    Canadian confederate cruiser : the story of the steamer Queen Victoria / John G. Langley.

    Includes bibliographical references and index.
    Issued in print and electronic formats.
    ISBN 978-1-77108-660-8 (hardcover).—ISBN 978-1-77108-661-5 (HTML)

    1. Queen Victoria (Ship)--History. I. Title.

VM383.Q5L36 2018   387.2'43   C2018-902874-2
                                            C2018-902875-0

 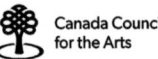

Nimbus Publishing acknowledges the financial support for its publishing activities from the Government of Canada, the Canada Council for the Arts, and from the Province of Nova Scotia. We are pleased to work in partnership with the Province of Nova Scotia to develop and promote our creative industries for the benefit of all Nova Scotians.

To the late Rear Admiral Hugh Francis Pullen, OBE, whose passion for maritime history, the untold story of the steamer *Queen Victoria*, and the important role she played in Canada's Confederation, was the inspiration for this book.

Table of Contents

Foreword by Ian McNaught   6
Preface   7

Part I – *Queen Victoria*, Ship of State

Chapter 1: The St. Lawrence: Great River of Canada   11
Chapter 2: Mr. Baby's Steamers   23
Chapter 3: *Queen Victoria*: Provincial Steamer to Royal Yacht   35

Part II – The Canadian Confederate Cruiser: Steaming Towards a New Nation

Chapter 4: Not Yet a Nation: Maritime Union or Confederation?   51
Chapter 5: North and South: The *Tallahassee* Affair   63
Chapter 6: Circus Act in Charlottetown   73
Chapter 7: Assault on Charlottetown   83
Chapter 8: Mopping Up: Quebec Conference   93

Part III – Attempts to Repatriate Canada's Liberty Bell

Chapter 9: The Last Voyage of *Queen Victoria*   107
Chapter 10: Rescue and Retribution   119
Chapter 11: An Important Gesture   129
Chapter 12: Canada's Liberty Bell   145

Epilogue: For Whom the Bell Tolls   155
Acknowledgments   161
Appendix 1: Short Biographies for Fathers of Confederation   165
Appendix 2: Biography of Rear Admiral Hugh Francis Pullen   175
Selected Bibliography   177
Bibliography   181
Image Credits   185
Index   187

TEL: 020 - 7481 6902
FAx: 020 - 7480 7662
email: deputy.master@thls.org
www.trinityhouse.co.uk

DEPUTY MASTER
CAPTAIN IAN MCNAUGHT **MNM**

Trinity House

TRINITY HOUSE,
TOWER HILL,
LONDON, EC3N 4DH

The maritime community, although spread right around the world and with a long history, is linked throughout its story in so many ways, and this book is no exception to that rule.

I first visited Montreal as a cadet on my first ship, MV *British Beech*, a product tanker of the BP Tanker Co. Fleet. Many years later my last visit to the mighty St. Lawrence was as the final Master on board the Cunard liner, *Queen Elizabeth 2*, and to add to the pleasure of that voyage in 2008 we had the splendid company of the author of this book, Mr. John Langley on-board. Once *QE2* was retired from service I became Master of Cunard's *Queen Victoria* and that name takes me straight back to Robert Napier and his steam tug, *Queen Victoria*, built in 1856 at Govan on the River Clyde. Robert Napier had already established links with Samuel Cunard and played an integral part with his ship designs and building in the establishment of the British and Northern American Royal Mail Steam Packet Co., later to become Cunard Line.

Now as I sit at my desk at Trinity House, Tower Hill, London, as the present Deputy Master, there are even more links with the gulf and river St. Lawrence. Like us in 1514, but somewhat later, Quebec Trinity House was set up in 1805, along with Montreal Trinity House in 1832, to ensure safe navigation and good pilotage and also to perform a maritime judicial role. Such roles ensure the safety of our waterways and vital links to the rest of the world and it is an honour for me to have played a small part in our shared maritime history, a history with an exciting, varied, and colourful story which I commend to you here in this book.

Ian McNaught.

March 2017

The Corporation of Trinity House is a Registered Charity

Preface

This book has been nearly ten years in the making. I am glad that it took this long because, had it not, the full story of the steamer *Queen Victoria* might not have been told.

On September 23, 2008, dawn was just breaking, and I stood shivering on the open deck of the *Queen Elizabeth 2* as she approached Quebec City on the St. Lawrence River. Very few passengers were about at that early hour. The teak decks were slick and wet from a heavy dew; the air was cold, just above freezing; and whirls of mist occasionally obstructed my view of the river. The eastern horizon was a riot of colour. As the shore quietly slipped by, church spires and white houses were back-dropped by pink and orange hues cast by the rising sun. Magical.

The voyage up the St. Lawrence River via the Gulf of St. Lawrence had been an eye-opener for passengers aboard QE2, most of whom were experiencing it for the first time. They were left with an indelible impression of majestic size and grandeur—fitting for a queen.

I knew a little about the steamer *Queen Victoria*, just enough for her to feature in my thoughts that morning. As Quebec City, the "Gibraltar of North America," loomed ahead, I reflected upon our safe passage upriver, which was due in part to the role played so many years earlier by the tug steamer *Queen Victoria* while in the service of Trinity House of Quebec. There was a story here, and I resolved there and then to write it—sometime.

Little did I know then how much more expansive the story would become as I furthered my research in the years that followed. Nor did I know then that just above where I stood that morning, Captain Ian McNaught, who was engaged in conversation with the pilot on the bridge of QE2, would write the foreword to this book in a role he later assumed as deputy master of Trinity House UK. Quite unbeknownst to me, the stars still visible in that early-morning sunrise, were aligning.

The saga of the *Queen Victoria* is really a compendium of stories. She had a very short lifespan of just ten years, but in that brief time she steamed unwittingly on a course and ultimately assumed the role of flagship of the emerging nation of Canada.

Queen Victoria and her sister ship, *Napoleon III*, were launched into service in 1856 as provincial tug steamers on the St. Lawrence River and home-ported in Quebec. Their very names evoke images of the "two nations"—one predominantly French and the other English—which reflected the historical evolution in British North America to that time, and the two founding nations which soon thereafter became the Dominion of Canada.

Queen Victoria excelled in her early days as a work boat, and together with *Napoleon III* played a major role in making the St. Lawrence safe for ships and shipping. Indeed, they were the forerunners of the Canadian Coast Guard. However, it was in her role as a "royal yacht," transporting monarchy and representatives of the Crown about the St. Lawrence River that *Queen Victoria* attained her most lasting reputation, and subsequently maritime immortality, as floating hotel and transport for the Canadian Fathers of Confederation.

That should have been more than enough of a legacy for any vessel. But *Queen Victoria* had, and has, another life that has reached up from the seabed of the Atlantic, which became her final resting place during a vicious hurricane in 1866. The story, like the ship, lay dormant for almost a century before slowly surfacing. It is a tale of sacrifice, seamanship, and raw emotion. All revolving around a ship's bell—the very bell from the *Queen Victoria*.

In recent years, as this part of her latent story has evolved, the *Queen Victoria* has come to symbolize common heritage, and just perhaps, nationalism. This steamer—a relatively small ship—occupies a significant place on the mantel of Canadian Confederation.

A note to the reader: despite every effort to sustain consistency, spelling is bound to vary due to the historic nature of the text and inevitable variations in quoted excerpts.

John G. Langley, QC
Baddeck, Nova Scotia

Part 1

Queen Victoria, Ship of State

CHAPTER 1

The St. Lawrence: Great River of Canada

In 1534, French explorer Jacques Cartier set sail from his home port of Saint-Malo, France, with a commission from King Francis I to seek a western passage to the wealthy markets of Asia under the now-famous royal commission "to discover certain islands and lands where it is said that a great quantity of gold and other precious things are to be found." He failed in that mission, but on this and two successive voyages he became the first European to describe and map the Gulf of St. Lawrence and the shores of the St. Lawrence River. He named the area "Country of Canadas" and claimed what is now part of Canada for France. The rest, they say, is history—our history.

The St. Lawrence is one of the greatest rivers in the world, an assertion fully endorsed by the renowned Canadian author Hugh MacLennan. He is reported to have said that "the St. Lawrence has made nations. It has been the moulder of lives of millions of people, perhaps by now hundreds of millions, in a multitude of different ways.... [It is] the greatest inland traffic avenue the world has ever known."

The river, its grand estuary—among the deepest and largest in the world—and the Gulf of St. Lawrence combine with the Great Lakes to form a hydrographic system that extends 2,500 miles into the heart of North America. The river begins as an extended arm of Lake Ontario, flowing east through the spectacular Thousand Islands near Gananoque, past Brockville, Prescott, Morrisburg, Cornwall, and on down to Montreal. From here and continuing to Trois-Rivières the

Jacques Cartier

Taking on the pilot, dawn on the St. Lawrence River.

river is calm, but from this point onwards to Quebec City, the freshwater flow becomes reversible with the tides. The distance from Montreal to Quebec City is 150 miles, a segment which historically is referred to as the upper St. Lawrence. From Quebec City east to the gulf is generally referred to as the lower St. Lawrence.

At Quebec City, the river constricts, and just past the city it divides to encircle Île d'Orléans, and then gradually widens with the waters becoming more brackish and tidal. The riverbed changes dramatically near the mouth of the Saguenay River, where the water depth drops from an average of seventy-five feet to one thousand feet. At Pointe-des-Monts, about forty miles east of Baie-Comeau, the north shore turns radically north-northeast towards Sept-Îles, effectively doubling the width of the river to over sixty miles.

According to the Royal Proclamation of 1763, a line drawn from the north shore at the mouth of the Rivière Saint-Jean, thence south past the west tip of Anticosti Island to Cap des Rosiers on the Gaspé Peninsula marks the end of the river and the beginning of the gulf. Pointe-des-Monts on the north shore has, in practice, been accepted as the western limit of the Gulf of St. Lawrence, and the beginning of the massive St. Lawrence River estuary, which extends from Île d'Orléans, downriver about two hundred miles to Point-des-Monts, where it widens into the Gulf of St. Lawrence.

The St. Lawrence River is entered by the gulf via the narrow Strait of Belle Isle, off the northern tip of Newfoundland, and, further south, through the Cabot Strait, which separates Cape Breton, Nova Scotia, from the southwestern coast of Newfoundland. The Gulf of St. Lawrence is a large body of water, a sea in fact, covering more than sixty thousand square miles. Half the ten provinces of Canada, to wit, New Brunswick,

Nova Scotia, Prince Edward Island, Newfoundland and Labrador, and Quebec, adjoin this body of water.

What began with Cartier's discovery in 1534 was continued seventy-four years later by another French explorer, Samuel de Champlain. It was the well-travelled Champlain who founded New France and Quebec City on July 3, 1608. Apart from his skills as a navigator, he was an accomplished cartographer, draftsman, and diplomat. In the years immediately before founding Quebec City, Champlain had, in 1604, explored and helped settle what would later become Saint John, New Brunswick, and in 1605 Port-Royal in Acadia, what we now know as Annapolis Royal, Nova Scotia.

Quebec City, where Champlain died in 1635, is one of the oldest cities in North America. Its name is derived from the Algonquin word *kebec*, meaning "where the river narrows," as does the St. Lawrence between the city's promontory Cap Diamant (Cape Diamond) and the city of Lévis on the opposite bank. The Historic District of Old Quebec with its distinct Upper and Lower Towns was declared a World Heritage Site by UNESCO in 1985.

In the years after its founding, Quebec City gradually grew and flourished, initially on the fur trade and later on timber exports. As the local economy thrived and expanded, so did the use of the St. Lawrence River. By 1800, Quebec City (Stadacona) and the upriver city of Montreal (Hochelaga) had developed into formidable centres of trade and commerce on the St. Lawrence.

The types of watercraft to be found on the river by this time were many and varied. They included canoes, which to this day are used and create great excitement during the annual winter race across the ice of the frozen river between Lévis and Quebec City. A flat-bottomed skiff or *bateau*, capable of carrying four or five tons of cargo, eventually became a more popular mode of transport. This concept was greatly expanded upon with the appearance of barges; with lengths of up to ninety feet, these increased the cargo-carrying capacity. Rafts and ferries were in great abundance. Sailing vessels later appeared and, before the advent of steam, made Quebec City the main *entrepôt* on the river, as the progress further upriver by ships of sail was impeded by the St. Mary's current at Montreal. The introduction of steam to the river would change all this, and very quickly with it the economic fortunes of Quebec City in favour of the cosmopolitan city of Montreal.

The Montreal beer baron John Molson manufactured the first steamship to work the St. Lawrence River. In 1809, the *Accommodation* completed her maiden voyage from Montreal to Quebec City and was the first in a succession of tug steamers that would revolutionize transportation and ship movements on the river. Henceforth, sailing vessels subject to the vagaries of wind, weather, and tide could be towed upriver to their ultimate destination. The result was a great expansion in commercial traffic, which coincidentally brought about a pressing need for new rules and regulations governing navigation and pilotage.

At this time, Quebec City was the capital of Lower Canada, or what later became the Province of Quebec. It was a colony of Britain, along with Upper Canada (Ontario) and the Maritime provinces of Nova Scotia, New Brunswick, and Prince Edward Island. As such the merchants and politicians of Quebec City sought the experience and counsel of Britain in addressing the pressing need to regulate traffic and protect shipping on the St. Lawrence River.

In 1514, some twenty years before Jacques Cartier first found his way into the St. Lawrence, Britain had grappled with a similar challenge and increasingly urgent need to provide a means to improve navigation and protect shipping around its own coast. Henry VIII was the reigning monarch, and by this time war and commerce had increased the volume of shipping on the River Thames to the point that the need for pilotage and safe conduct became paramount to the Port of London.

On March 19, 1513, a guild of mariners, troubled by the inexperience and poor conduct of unregulated pilots on the Thames endangering life and cargo, petitioned the king for licence to set up a fraternity enabled to regulate pilotage on the capital's river. The petitioners were very well prepared and advanced the following case to the king:

> *The practice of pilotship in rivers, by young men who are unwilling to take the labour and adventure of learning the shipman's craft on the high seas, is likely to cause scarcity of mariners; and so this your realm which heretofore hath flourished with a navy to all other lands dreadful, shall be left destitute of cunning masters and mariners; also the Scots, Flemings and Frenchmen have been*

suffered to learn as loadsmen (pilots) the secrets of the King's streams, and in time of war have come as far as Gravesende and set owte English shippes to the great rebuke of the realm.

Henry VIII was duly impressed, and on May 20, 1514, he signed the Royal Charter incorporating that body of mariners as "the Master, Wardens and Assistants of the Guild or Fraternity of the most glorious and individible Trinity and St. Clement in the Parish Church of Deptford Strond," a name that mercifully was later shortened to Trinity House. With respect to the name chosen for this fraternity, the word "Trinity" refers to the Holy Trinity, St. Clement to the patron saint of mariners, and Deptford at that time was the hub of transactions for the Port of London.

This new corporation was to be governed by a master, four wardens, and eight assistants who were to be elected annually, and were empowered for the general improvement of the science of navigation, to elect and expel any of their number; by-laws could be created, and transgressors punished by forfeit or expulsion. A seal served as the legal mark, and the corporation was authorized to hold property to conduct its charitable affairs and meetings, with a chaplain appointed to pray for the kings, queens, and brethren living and deceased.

To this day, the corporation is headed by the master whose extensive powers and jurisdiction are deferred to the deputy master. The first master of Trinity House UK was Sir Thomas Spert, master of the *Mary Rose*, flagship of King Henry VIII. In more recent times, the role of master has become largely ceremonial and filled by members of the royal family. Prince Philip, Duke of Edinburgh served as master from 1969 until 2011, when he relinquished that role to Princess Anne, Princess Royal, the current master.

The deputy master is the executive of the corporation, presiding at board and court meetings, and expected to arrange all the business for the consideration of the court. Today this position is held by Captain Ian McNaught, who previously served with Cunard Line as the last master of the flagship *Queen Elizabeth 2*.

Trinity House UK today is ruled by thirty-one Elder Brethren, who are appointed from three hundred Younger Brethren, and act as advisors and perform other duties as needed. The Younger Brethren are generally lay people with maritime experience, often ship's masters, naval officers, pilots, and yachtsmen. As originally constituted, Trinity House to this day carries out three primary functions. First, it is the

Deputy Master Ian McNaught with Princess Anne, Master of Trinity House UK.

official General Lighthouse Authority for England, Wales, the Channel Islands, and Gibraltar, responsible for the provision and maintenance of navigational aids, lighthouses, light vessels, and buoys as well as radio and satellite communication systems. Second, it is the official Deep Sea Pilotage Authority and as such provides expert navigators for ships trading in northern European waters. Finally, Trinity House is a maritime charity, disbursing funds for the welfare of retired seamen, the training of young cadets, and the promotion of safety at sea.

Trinity House UK has a long and storied history. It celebrated its four hundredth anniversary in 1914. The following tribute appeared in *Lloyd's List* in May of that year and said simply: "As a matter of history the record of Trinity House is fascinating. In its time it has been many sided. It has served the nation in this capacity and that, and all the while it has somehow managed to make itself so indispensable that, in an age of scant reverence for ancient institutions, it stands not only unassailed, but, we might also add, unassailable." Yet another century would pass, when in 2014 Trinity House celebrated its quincentenary—five hundred years of service to a grateful nation as one of Britain's oldest and most singular institutions.

At the dawn of the nineteenth century in the colonies, shipping traffic had greatly increased on the St. Lawrence River. As had been the case in Britain, increasingly there was a need for some form of control and oversight to protect shipping from the Gulf of St. Lawrence and upriver to Montreal via Quebec City. The ensuing "Trinity House movement"

in the Province of Quebec would bring about the extension to the St. Lawrence of officially disciplined navigation, in much the same manner as happened in Britain nearly three hundred years earlier.

So it was, using Trinity House in the mother country as a model, that the Trinity House of Quebec was established in 1805. The corporation was an autonomous body under the government of the Province of Lower Canada. It was created by an Act of Provincial Parliament, "with full power and authority to make, ordain and constitute such and so many by-laws, Rules and Orders, not repugnant to the maritime laws of Great Britain or to the laws of this province...for the more convenient, safe and easy navigation of the River Saint Lawrence, from the fifth rapid above the City of Montreal, downwards, as well by the laying down as taking up of buoys and anchors, as by the erecting of lighthouses, beacons or landmarks, the clearing of sands or rocks or otherwise howsoever."

As originally constituted, the Trinity House of Quebec was governed by a master, a deputy master, two wardens appointed in Quebec and three in Montreal (which initially was a subordinate branch of the parent body), as well as various officers. Its first appointments included: Master Honourable John Stewart; Deputy Master H. LeMesurier; Wardens Honourable George Pemberton, David Burnet, G. B. Symes, Harbour Master John Lambly, and Superintendent of Pilots Robert Young. The officers included E. B. Lindsay and George Manly Muir (clerk and registrar), Errol B. Lindsay (treasurer), Assistant Harbour Master and Superintendent of cul-de-sac William K. Rayside; B. Simon, alias LaFleur, (water bailiff); and Pierre Rodrigue, messenger and wharfinger.

When created in 1805, Trinity House of Quebec was conceived to maintain order at the growing port of Quebec City, which up until that time was the upstream limit of sailing navigation for ocean-going ships. Steam had yet to appear on the scene. Between 1790 and 1810, ship traffic greatly increased as the wood and timber trade overtook furs as Quebec's primary export.

Shipping on the St. Lawrence was seasonal—the river froze up during the winter months. During the shipping season all manner of vessels plied the river—fishing sloops, tugboats, barges, horse-drawn ferries, rowboats, canoes, and soon steamers. Trinity House of Quebec wardens regulated all this traffic. As originally incorporated, Trinity House of Quebec had responsibility to look after lights and buoys from Montreal to the Strait of Belle Isle, or virtually the entire upper and lower St. Lawrence. This was no mean task. In addition, the corporation issued pilot's licences, looked after lights and buoys in the St. Lawrence River, and dealt with criminal matters. It quickly assumed and maintained a dominant role as overseer of the St. Lawrence.

Some years later, as the upriver port of Montreal prospered and grew, a Trinity House of Montreal was established by similar legislation enacted in February of 1832. It too was based on the British model with much the same governance as the Quebec operation. Henceforth, Trinity House of Montreal was able to make its own laws, license pilots, appoint harbour masters, clerks, and bailiffs. Its jurisdiction included the upper St. Lawrence and the port of Montreal (thus relieving Quebec of that responsibility), within which area it was to place lights, buoys, and other aids to navigation. Like Quebec, it also had a quasi-judicial role by which it could hear disputes between the masters of ships and pilots and complaints between pilots and harbour authorities. Upon inception it was managed by Master Robert Armour; Deputy Master Jules Quesnel; Wardens John Molson, William Edmonstone, H. L. Routh, John Try, and Andrew Shaw; officers Hypolite Guy (registrar and treasurer) and John N. Ogilvy (water bailiff).

The following advertisement, which appeared August 22, 1811, in the *Quebec Gazette* newspaper, provides a typical example of how the Quebec and Montreal Trinity Houses carried out their mandate of regulating and licensing pilots: "Antoine Roussel, Pilot, for and below the harbor of Quebec was suspended and rendered incapable of piloting any ship or vessel, for and during the term of six months, and of any of His Majesty's ships or vessels for a term of two years, being convicted of having, from a want of knowledge of the channel, run the *AMELIA*, frigate, the Hon. Frederick Paul Irby, Captain, on the middle ground in the traverse opposite to the point of Saint Roe's on the 20th of June last.' Sgd: William Lindsay, Jr, Registrar, Trinity House Quebec."

Due to the political realities associated with the emergence of a new nation, these two authorities would not experience quite the longevity of their British role model. However, they would prove worthy of their namesake in London, co-operating fully with the Admiralty, the Imperial Boards of Trade, and the various boards of lighthouse commissioners in the Atlantic provinces, to be succeeded only at Confederation in 1867 by the newly created Department of Marine and Fisheries in the new Dominion of Canada. Confederation, however, was still a long way off, and by that time, the Trinity Houses of Quebec and Montreal had created an enduring legacy as "Good Samaritans of the St. Lawrence."

Quebec City from Citadel, circa 1836.

The emergence of steam-powered vessels revolutionized shipping and transportation on the St. Lawrence in the early 1800s. John Molson's tug steamboat *Accommodation* was quickly followed by a succession of steam tugs, all vying for supremacy in the lucrative tugboat trade. In the early years, the Montreal-based Molson and Torrance families dominated this market, creating a virtual monopoly before later merging their firms.

Their counterpart in Quebec City was an entrepreneur by the name of Charles François Xavier Baby. The Baby family had deep roots in Lower Canada dating back to the days of the earliest settlements in New France. François Baby, as he was known, was the eldest of a family of twelve children and seemed destined for business. He had mixed success with his foray into the timber trade and, by times, bordered on bankruptcy—all of which belied the reality of the prominent businessman he would become in succeeding years.

In 1841, the provinces of Upper Canada (Ontario) and Lower Canada (Quebec) were united to form the new Province of Canada. The predominantly anglophone Ontario subsequently was referred to as Canada West, while the francophone province of Quebec was dubbed Canada East, a political demarcation that would remain in place until 1867.

Baby was well-connected in government circles in Quebec, much like his father before him. In the early 1850s, he received a series of contracts from the government and Trinity House of Quebec for the building and maintaining of lighthouses on the lower St. Lawrence. This would prove to be a monumental task, which over the course of the next few years, saw Baby oversee construction of four Imperial Lighthouses in the Gulf of St. Lawrence.

At this time the greatly increased use of the gulf and St. Lawrence River—largely brought about by revolutionary changes in steam technology—had already rendered obsolete many of the navigation aids on the St. Lawrence. Lobbying by shipping interests and the Admiralty resulted in an ambitious three-year building program for lighthouses wherein Great Britain would bear all materials and construction costs. The so-called Imperial Lights were tall conical structures, resembling the British style based on the Stevenson design. They were made of brick or masonry; in some cases the granite was quarried and prepared by Scottish stonemasons and shipped to the colony as ballast.

Baby had a modest fleet of small steam tugs at the time, which he was able to employ transporting men and materials to the lighthouse construction sites. They included the *Admiral* and the *Alert*. The challenges confronting the builder were formidable. Cap des Rosiers, situated near the tip of the Gaspé Peninsula, marks the turning point from the Gulf of St. Lawrence into the St. Lawrence River. It was named by Samuel de Champlain for the abundance of wild roses in the area, in stark contrast to the history of this promontory, which has produced more shipwrecks than any other area of the Gaspésie. The tower and the dwelling were to have been completed by September 1, 1854, but these were delayed considerably due to the unavailability of local stone. When ultimately completed in 1857, and with the lantern in place, the tower reached a total height of 112 feet, making it the tallest lighthouse ever built in Canada. Construction costs approximated $115,000. Cap des Rosiers was declared a National Historic Site in 1974. The tower was designated a Classified Federal Heritage Building in 1994.

The Strait of Belle Isle, which runs between Newfoundland and Labrador for a distance of approximately ninety-four miles, links the Atlantic to the Gulf of St. Lawrence and lies along the shortest route between the cities on the St. Lawrence and England. Before steam became dominant, sailing vessels often took the longer route between Cape Breton and the south shore of Newfoundland. While adding about

Modern pilot boat, Quebec City.

two hundred miles to the voyage, the route was much wider and free of icebergs and strong currents.

The advent of the steamship, however, made more captains willing to pass through the Strait of Belle Isle. Belle Isle itself, French for "beautiful island," is anything but. Neither is it large at twelve miles in length and two miles wide. Apparently, Jacques Cartier was so unimpressed with the island's bleak landscape in the spring of 1534 that he described it as "the land God gave Cain." John Page, chief engineer of public works for Canada, described Belle Isle as "consisting of a range of bare, rocky hills, without a tree, shrub or grassy spot being visible on their rugged surfaces."

With increased usage, the Province of Canada determined to build two lighthouses to mark the strait—one on the southwestern tip of Belle Isle near the eastern side of the strait and another at Pointe Amour on the Labrador coast, near the opposite end of the strait where it constricts to a mere nine miles. Construction of both provided Baby with many challenges—perhaps more so in the case of the light at the "south end, upper" on Belle Isle. Just to get ashore proved difficult. In order to get to the worksite, Baby and twenty-two workmen, once they landed in a small bay near the southern end of the island, had to first construct a road nearly one and a half miles in length that cut through granite outcroppings as it snaked up a circuitous ravine.

One can only imagine the conditions for the workmen who overwintered during 1855–1856 to complete the construction. To add yet more misery, the tug steamer *Doris*, carrying fodder for the horses engaged in the construction work, wrecked on the island in 1856. As the island produced no vegetation of any description for the horses, the Province of Canada's commissioner of public works reported, "The poor brutes were thus starved and before relieved by death from their sufferings, became mad and attempted to devour one another."

The lighthouse on Anticosti Island—West Point Light—was yet another test of the perseverance and tenacity of Baby and his workmen. Anticosti Island has been popularly described as "a massive tongue of limestone protruding from the mouth of the St. Lawrence River, swept by strong currents, buffeted by treacherous winds and ringed by reefs that stretched some two miles offshore." It was these same reefs that made it very difficult to unload supply boats, which often were obliged to lie off the island for typically four or five days at a time before they could be unloaded by boats from the island. Here, too, the workmen overwintered during 1855–1856 under the harshest of conditions in order to complete the beautiful brick and stone tower.

For François Baby, just to complete the construction of these lighthouses was a significant accomplishment. They quickly proved their worth and greatly enhanced navigation in the Gulf of St. Lawrence. So impressed was Chief Engineer John Page that of these four lights he was quoted as having said, "Indeed, greater attention and care have been bestowed on the respective structures to render their stability certain than I ever expected, when there were so many difficulties to contend with…and in my opinion, the contractor (Baby) is not only entitled to credit for the manner in which the work has been performed, but should be allowed a fair and reasonable profit on the expenditure, as the prosecution of the work has been far more onerous and perplexing than any human foresight could possibly have anticipated."

During ongoing efforts to improve navigational aids with new lighthouses, it was also apparent that towage and salvage services on the St. Lawrence were inferior to meet the needs of the day. To that end, the commissioner of public works advised the government that tenders should be called for the provision of a superior class of tugboats, both for the increasing speed of sailing ships making the gulf and for general duties in a government marine service.

The successful bidder was François Baby. The new Baby steamers, as they were known, would greatly influence shipping and navigation on the St. Lawrence—and take their place in the history of an emerging Canadian nation.

CHAPTER 2

Mr. Baby's Steamers

Britain might be excused for any impression of having little time for colonial affairs during the 1850s. At this time the nation was preoccupied with involvement in the Crimean War as an ally with France, the Ottoman Empire, and Sardinia against Russia. The conflict was fought far from home, in the Crimea and Balkans, from October 1853 until the peace accord with Russia in March of 1856.

This was an extraordinary period in the relationship between Britain and France. Just a few years earlier, both countries had been bitter enemies in a war that ultimately ended with the surrender and exile of French emperor Napoleon I. Much had changed since 1815, in both England and France. In 1837, Queen Victoria, the daughter of Prince Edward, Duke of Kent ascended the throne and, at the age of eighteen became Queen of the United Kingdom of Great Britain and Ireland. Thus began a sixty-three-year reign known as the Victorian era. It was a tenure many thought would never be replicated or exceeded. (The pundits have proven to be wrong, as Queen Elizabeth II, the current reigning monarch, is presently enjoying her sixty-fifth year of reign with every sign of continued good health.)

Meanwhile in France, yet another Napoleon appeared on the political scene. The nephew and heir of Napoleon I, Louis-Napoleon Bonaparte ascended the throne as Emperor Napoleon III in December of 1852. Interestingly, he was an Anglophile, having spent a good deal of time in England prior to taking over the reins of government in France. He and his wife, Empress Eugenie, whom he married in January of 1853, became very good friends with Queen Victoria and her husband, Albert, whom she

Napoleon III

Queen Victoria

had wed in 1840. The friendship was a somewhat natural outcome of the allied relationship of both countries in the Crimean War. It blossomed into something considerably more thereafter, to a point where it was described as a "grande entente."

Both heads of state in the years following the anointing of the new French emperor vied for bragging rights as to who could extend more invitations to the other to visit their country. No expense was spared in providing entertainment and lavish dining for the visiting heads of state in both England and France. Both Napoleon III and Queen Victoria and their respective spouses were adored by countrymen in France and England.

It was during the time François Baby was preparing a response to the government tug tender in Quebec City that Napoleon III and his wife were guests of Queen Victoria and Albert in England, on April 17-21, 1855. While in London on April 19, Napoleon III, effusing about the accord between the two countries, was quoted as saying, "The interests of the two countries were everywhere identical." These remarks were addressed to an army and navy that had been engaged in a "united companionship of danger and gallantry," and also addressed the two governments, both of whom he trusted were based on "truth, moderation and justice."

The *Glasgow Herald* newspaper reported this royal visit was a "week of splendor," which could be described as an "entente cordiale," and on the subject of Napoleon III, "one motive seems to have activated him and that was to prove how genuine his feelings of amity were towards the British nation....The friendship towards each other which was displayed by the royal personages during the ovation of last week was manifested as strongly towards them by the crowds who hailed them wherever they went, and we are pleased to regard the events of those brilliant days as the first fruits of what all good men, on both sides of St. George's Channel hope may be an enduring and holy alliance between the peoples."

Napoleon III had hardly returned to his native soil when he felt compelled to return the invitation. A few months later, in August 1855, Victoria and Albert, along with their children, would be guests of the emperor in France. At Calais, where the royal party would first step upon French soil, the preparations were being made in earnest. This was closely followed by the British media, which reported, "The City of Calais which has already received within its walls almost all the crowned heads of Europe will never have offered a nobler and more sympathetic reception than that which awaited the august ally of France."

The emperor—and France—did not disappoint. During their nine-day state visit to France, Queen Victoria and Albert were feted like no other heads of state in living memory. Napoleon had personally organized the program of events, which included visits to the Universal Exhibition, the Louvre, Versailles, Sainte-Chapelle, and Notre-Dame. For the culmination of the royal tour a magnificent dinner for 2,500 guests was held in the Salle de l'Opéra at the Château de Versailles on August 25. Later, Queen Victoria would describe in her journal this particular event as "one of the most beautiful and majestic evenings they had ever attended." At this time in history, relations between Britain and France had never been better.

Back across the English Channel, the summer of 1855 had also marked a milestone in maritime history. On July 3, the largest and most technologically advanced Atlantic steamship was launched on the River Clyde in Scotland to the delight of more than fifty thousand spectators. She was christened as RMS *Persia*, the newest flagship of the Cunard Line. The *Illustrated London News* described her as "the most magnificent floating hotel and goods transport that has ever breasted the waters."

One headline in the *Glasgow Herald* on July 4, 1855, described the previous day's event as "Launch of Cunard Liner Persia: The Largest Steamer in the World." From the building yard of Robert Napier & Sons of Govan:

> The event came off successfully in the presence of an immense concourse of applauding spectators. The Messrs Napier, to whose eminence as marine architects and engineers we need not advert, are the builders of both the hull and the engines. Miss Wilson of Dundyvan had the honour of naming this the largest ship afloat. Lord Provost presided over the grand reception at which the Messrs

> *Burns were present. One thousand ladies and gentlemen guests after the launch returned to the drawing room connected with the works, and on the floor on which the proportions of all these great (Cunard) ships are first chaulked out, were treated to a sumptuous champagne lunch. Lord Provost proposed a toast to Robert Napier who, in replying, cordially thanked his Lordship for proposing his health, and, (modest man that he was), he might state that his son had been the principal instrument in performing the work. He mentioned this because he thought that young people more especially should get the honour when they deserved it.*

The mastermind behind construction of the first of Cunard's iron steamships was the renowned Scottish marine engineer Robert Napier. He was born at Dumbarton in 1791 at the height of the Industrial Revolution, which by his time had helped establish the River Clyde as the best location for shipbuilding in the British Empire. By the time of the *Persia* launch, Napier had already engined or built some forty steam vessels for Cunard Line, in which he was a principal partner along with founder Samuel Cunard of Halifax, Nova Scotia; George Burns of Glasgow, Scotland; and David McIver of Liverpool, England. This partnership was his greatest success and largely contributed to the reputation he achieved during his lifetime as Father of Clyde Shipbuilding.

Robert Napier was frequently consulted and respected by governments all over Europe, particularly France. He was a juror at the Crystal Palace Great Exhibition—the first of the world's fair exhibitions of culture and industry—at London, England, in 1851. He served in a similar capacity at the Paris Exhibition in 1855 and was appointed a chevalier of the Légion d'honneur by Napoleon III, who by then had become a personal friend. That friendship had blossomed even further by 1867, when Napoleon III made Napier a royal commissioner of the Paris Exhibition (the second to be hosted by Paris), and presented him to Empress Eugenie.

The *Persia* had been three years in the planning and construction. Napier, always a stickler for details, wanted to get it right. Nothing was spared, no corners cut in the construction. Following her launch, and while she was still being fitted out, Napier entered into negotiations in the summer of 1855 for the construction of two steam tugboats with François Baby from Quebec City. Just how Baby was able to prevail upon Napier to build his comparatively modest steamships remains a mystery.

Having just launched the largest and most challenging undertaking in the *Persia*, Napier was tired and considering the prospects of retirement. He was also in negotiations with the British Admiralty for the design and construction of a new type of "bomb ship," encouraged by the French for use in the Crimean War. Retirement would have to wait.

The Department of Public Works tender called for two steamers to be especially designed for Canadian service as lighthouse and buoy tenders. They were also to be designed as estuary tugs for sailing ships, with the ability to handle passenger and freight service to the lower St. Lawrence. With such mixed duty specifications they might, under ordinary circumstances, have presented too much of a challenge to naval architects. Napier, whose reputation was well known in Quebec circles, would prove to be more than up to the task. The result would be two steamers, yard numbers 75 and 76, identical in every respect, and while small, were advanced for their time.

It was October 27, 1855, when Baby put forth his offer for his two ships. Napier accepted it the same day and agreed to have the vessels completed by July 1, 1856. The specifications called for two steam vessels fitted with single screw propellers to be employed as tugs at the mouth of the St. Lawrence River. They would be 170 feet long, 30 feet in breadth, and have a draft of 17½ feet. They both had flush decks with a straight-stemmed iron hull and "an extra strong plate forward strongly braced as a preservation against the ice for each vessel for about two feet above load draft to about two feet below light draft."

Napier was not a man to do half a job. Clearly he was prepared to put as much thought and effort into the smallest of steamers as the largest of Atlantic greyhounds. In this way he demonstrated to Baby what the British press had previously said of the builder: "What can be done by others is one thing, what has been done by Napier is another."

Each vessel had two boilers and thus two funnels with a natural draft. The engines, or the "Napier machinery," the best in the world, for both ships were rated at 250 horsepower by Admiralty rule, but were capable of producing upwards of 1,500 horsepower and a service speed of 13 knots. Each had galleys that could accommodate some 150 passengers and crew as well as food for immigrants while transferring from ocean ship to shore. There was sleeping accommodation for a modest number of passengers who could be transported in reasonable comfort. Passengers

Charles François Xavier Baby

were placed aft along with the captain and officers, where a large overhead awning provided cool comfort from the sun in summer as well as protection from cinders and funnel smoke.

Both steamers were splendid-looking vessels with their black hulls and funnels. Their deck work was varnished or painted and grained. It was still the practice to build ocean-going steamers with masts for sails to supplement engine power when conditions warranted. Baby's steamers were built in this fashion, each with two masts, although given the nature of these ships as tug steamers, it is likely that they seldom employed sails while in service.

True to his word, Napier delivered. *Queen Victoria* and *Napoleon III* were launched in 1856, May and June respectively. While no record has been found to explain the choice of vessel names, they clearly reflect the times, christened as they were with the names of the era's two most outstanding heads of state. It is no small irony either that the chosen names—one English and the other French—happened to reflect François Baby's culture and society back home in the Province of Canada.

The Baby contract pushed Napier to the limit. While in the midst of building the two Baby steamers, he had accepted a commission from the British Admiralty for a rush order to build the ironclad bomb ship *Erebus*. At this time, both Britain and France were allies in their effort to defeat Russia in the Crimea. Orders from the British Admiralty were clearly given preference, but it would seem not to the detriment of other ongoing contracts.

Accordingly, work on *Erebus* began in January of 1856, during which time the Napier yard was also engaged in the construction of both *Napoleon III* and *Queen Victoria*. In order to accommodate the Admiralty, work on the gunboat was pushed day and night with 1,200 men employed on her construction. In an incredible feat of both engineering and construction, *Erebus* was launched with her machinery on April 19, 1856, having been only three and a half months in the making! This remarkable turnaround was no doubt due in part to the £1,000 per diem penalty clause for late delivery written into the Admiralty contract.

The pressure on Napier must have been enormous: to finish up the fitting out of *Persia,* the largest ocean steamship ever built, while designing, constructing, and delivering two steamers for François Baby, and to design and build a radically new warship for the Admiralty—on time and on budget—and all in less than twelve months was almost unimaginable. As Robert Napier would attest, much of the credit for this exploit was due to his son James R. Napier. Indeed, the strain told severely on the latter's health, and he retired from the firm shortly thereafter. But not before father and son had lent their hands to ensure that a Napier-built tug steamer would go on to play an important role in the emergence of a new nation across the Atlantic, in British North America.

The newly minted *Queen Victoria* and *Napoleon III* left the Clyde in the late summer of 1856, bound for their new home at Quebec City on the St. Lawrence River. It was not to be a pleasure cruise but rather a "working passage" from Scotland to their destination. Upon arrival, they would join the other tugs in the Baby fleet, the *Admiral* and *Advance*, in their shared duties on the St. Lawrence.

Napoleon III was the first to arrive at Quebec City on September 8, 1856. She had come via Sydney, Cape Breton, and while en route had picked up a tow, the ship *Tehernaya*, which she brought up to Quebec City. It was a good omen to François Baby that his new tug tender made money for his company on its maiden voyage. Baby was justifiably proud of his newest vessel, and shortly after her arrival in Quebec City he invited the local press and business leaders to experience *Napoleon III* in a short cruise to nearby Grosse Isle.

The *Queen Victoria* was not far behind, arriving at Quebec City on September 20 under the command of Captain McKay. Soon after tying up, McKay oversaw the unloading of the remaining cargo, some of which was destined for Montreal and some—twelve cases, two casks, and two bales—for Mr. Baby. The remainder—twenty-one packages, three barrels of crockery, eight casks of wine, and six boxes of herrings—was consigned to a Mrs. Inglis.

Queen Victoria was the immediate subject of a good deal of interest in the local press. The following editorial summing up her first journey appeared in the September 22 edition of the *Quebec Gazette* under the title "The Second Tug-Steamship":

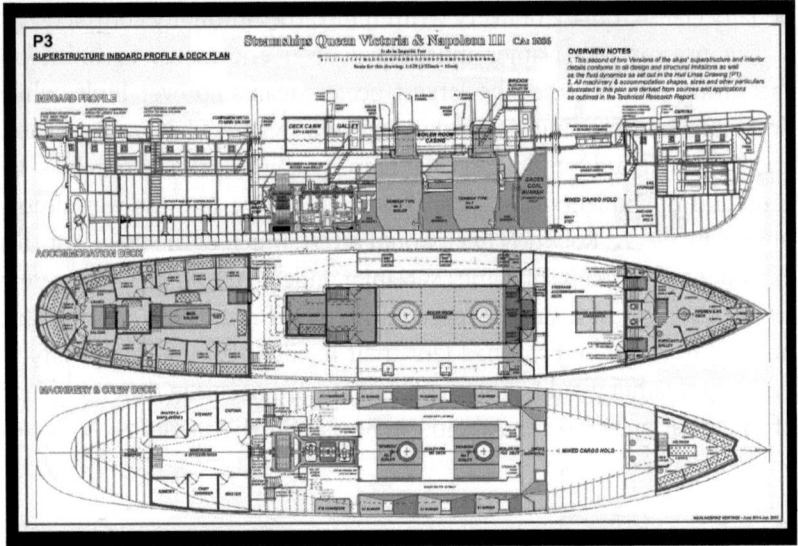

Blueprints of the steamer Queen Victoria.

The Queen Victoria, another of Mr. Baby's fine looking and powerful tug-steamships arrived in port Saturday evening about 6 o'clock. She is the twin sister of the Napoleon III. In appearance, horsepower and accommodation the two steamers are precisely alike. The Queen Victoria left the Clyde on the 14th for Havre, and having there shipped lighthouse materials went to Cork or Queenstown for coals to bring her to America.

That port she left on the 27th and experienced weather which only a first class sea boat could withstand. Intending to come through the Strait of Belle Isle to Quebec she made for the north coast of Newfoundland and there was detained 27 hours by fog, after which Captain McKay, perceiving that he had not coals enough to come up to Quebec, as he had to call at Cape Rosier and other places, ran through the strait for Sydney, Cape Breton to coal and arrived there on the 12th of September. There he took on 10 additional passengers—there were Mr. Nicholson of Cork and Mrs. Kinghorn of Glasgow previously on-board; and having coaled, steamed for Quebec, touching at Cape Rosier and remaining there for 10 hours landing lighthouse materials.

Both steamers immediately took up their duties on the lower St. Lawrence along with the other smaller Baby tug steamers *Advance*, then under the command of Captain Paul Pouliot, *Admiral*, under Captain Eugene Gourdeau. Baby wasted no time in advertising his new steamers. Despite the lateness of the season, the following advertisement appeared in the *Quebec Gazette* of October 1:

> PROVINCIAL TUG STEAMERS FOR
> THE LOWER SAINT LAWRENCE
> *The new iron screw tug steamers Napoleon III, Captain William Davidson and Queen Victoria, Captain David McKay have commenced their regular trips down the Saint Lawrence and will be found stationed at Brandy Pots and elsewhere for towing and otherwise assisting vessels.*

The advertisement is signed by the company agent on St. Peter Street, F. Buteau, who advised that he was prepared to receive all orders for towage, "which will meet with immediate attention."

At this time, the steamers were berthed at Atkinson's Wharf on the Quebec waterfront. The advertisements were evidently effective: the shipping news columns in the local press were immediately impressed by the newest additions to the Baby fleet. Although François Baby was not without his detractors, the local press was generally supportive, as exemplified by an editorial headlined "The Tug Steamships," which appeared in the *Quebec Gazette* on October 18:

> *Never before was an improvement suggested without being stoutly, earnestly and vigorously opposed. Steam, gas, electricity have, each in turn been vigorously resisted. As it has been with steam, gas and electricity in the abstract, so it is with Mr. Baby and the tug steam ships which he has placed upon the Saint Lawrence in particular. Private interests have exclaimed against tug steamships and against Mr. Baby because private interest was to be interfered with by public interest. Mr. Baby it has been said is a favourite and has obtained money from the government with which to fill a government contract. Mr. Baby too is a French Canadian; we are English and this is an English colony and we are neglected. Besides, of what use is it to send up vessels quickly to Quebec and send them off quickly? The longer they remain here, surely the better it is for the port. Such is the manner in which the opponents of almost every improvement reason.*

> *The President of the Board of Trade, Hon. Robert Lowe of London, England who was here a day or two ago did not however fail to perceive the advantages which Mr. Baby's new tug steamships must confer upon the port in rendering the approaches to it safe and easy....*
>
> *Steam, and the steam tug ships enable the intelligent mariner to escape shipwreck by taking as soon as possible a steamer instead of simply a pilot, because the steamer has a pilot—the cost of pilotage is included in the cost of towage, and the savings of tides and contrary winds in men's wages and food makes pilotage and towage amount to nothing. The seagoing public are already begun to give Mr. Baby a vote of confidence. That the advantages of the towing system is gaining upon seafaring people may be gathered from the fact that Mr. Baby's first boats, in one season, only towed nine ships, and the next, 18, while this year over 100 have been towed up and very many towed down.*
>
> *In truth, the work has been admirably performed—so much so indeed that no American shipmaster has ever refused a tow.*
>
> *Mr. Baby deserves reward for his enterprise and energy, and he will meet with it, and the public of Montreal and Quebec will yet have to thank him for being chiefly instrumental in the reduction of the premiums of insurance on ships coming to and leaving the Saint Lawrence.*

What skeptics and critics of François Baby were effusing over was the matter of government subsidies. Despite the bright future that Mr. Baby's new steamers promised for improved navigation and transportation on the St. Lawrence, the towage business—much like the ferry business of today—was soon found to require government subsidies in order to operate. This reality would give rise to a change in fortunes for François Baby. In the meantime however, a need to secure another purpose-built steamer for the St. Lawrence became apparent. Wisely, Baby looked to Robert Napier once again for help.

The result was the launch in 1857 of yet another Napier-built vessel, yard number 82, the provincial steamer *Lady Head*. The steamer was named after Anna Maria, Lady Head, the wife of Sir Edmund Walker

Head, who was Governor General of the United Province of Canada during the period 1854–1861. The vessel was a slightly smaller version of *Queen Victoria* and *Napoleon III*, having a length of 150 feet, beam of 24 feet, draft of 13 feet, and generating 150 horsepower. Her profile was similar, except with just one boiler she had just the one funnel. The fact that she was virtually identical in design to the two larger Baby steamers probably accounts for how quickly Napier was able to respond and complete this undertaking. She was built at a cost of £68,000.

Lady Head arrived at Quebec City in early July 1857, an event which the local media proclaimed, "She will for the present be in the employ of the Trinity House of Quebec and will be commanded by Captain William Davidson." She was primarily employed carrying passengers, mail, and goods between Canada (Quebec) and the Maritime provinces, or the lower provinces as they were called. *Queen Victoria* and her sister ship remained engaged primarily in government work and rarely were used commercially. Occasionally, however, *Queen Victoria* would fill in for *Lady Head* in the run downriver to Pictou, Nova Scotia, often for the last voyage of the season.

Lady Head would be the last steamer built for Baby. He would not live to see her demise in 1878, when she became a total loss, stranded near the Cap des Rosiers lighthouse—ironically the first of Baby's Imperial Lights.

CHAPTER 3

Queen Victoria: Provincial Steamer to Royal Yacht

In 1857, François Baby began his first full year of steamer tug service with the knowledge that the tariff rates for towage would be challenging to the shipping fraternity. On June 22, shortly after the season began and the river was open to shipping, he ran an advertisement for "Provincial Tug Steamers" in which he gave "NOTICE that from and after this day and until the 15th of October next, the TARIFF RATES for towage as established by Proclamation of His Excellency the Governor General are hereby reduced by 50 per cent."

This action, while appearing to be drastic, was in response to a growing resistance on the part of the shipping public to pay what many felt were overly onerous rates. What began initially as a murmur of protest, by later on in that year had become a rant of sorts, typified by this account from the *Quebec Gazette* of November 11, 1857, in which the paper reported on the recent stranding of the *Polynesia* in the St. Lawrence:

> The captain had left the ship (upon stranding) and returned to Quebec to hire a steamer to assist in getting his ship off, but he has not been able to get one at anything like a reasonable price. Mr. Baby's steamers are the only ones to be had now that are fit for the purpose and he asks £100 per day for the use of one, and should it come to a blow when the steamer gets to the ship, which is very likely at this boisterous season, she might have to lie there a week or more before she could land anything. This charge, together with the expense of "platforming" the ship and bringing her up would amount to more than she would be worth. The charge for the steamer really appears enormous when we consider that these boats are subsidized by government to assist vessels in distress. Nearly all Saint Lawrence River steamers have gone into winter quarters. This is much earlier than usual and we presume the hard times and stagnation of business have had much to do with the laying up of the vessels.

Such were the challenges Baby faced as he endeavoured to fulfill his government contract—and at the same time make a profit. It wasn't to be. Baby continued to operate and receive government subsidies for another year. By the summer of 1859, and despite the best efforts of both government and contractor, it was apparent that the service was being run at a loss and was not sustainable. The government accepted Baby's offer of his entire fleet, to abandon his contracts for towing and Trinity House work with lighthouses and beacons on terms mutually agreed upon between the two parties. All proceeds from the transfer in ownership would be put towards the retirement of Baby's substantial debts. These negotiations were confirmed by an Order-in-Council of August 1859 at which point Baby's five steamers, including *Queen Victoria* and *Napoleon III*, passed under the direct control of the commissioner of public works.

The sessional papers for the legislative assembly released in 1860 provide an interesting account of the financial arrangements made between the government and Baby during the term of his aborted contract: "RETURN showing the several sums paid from the Public Chest to Mr. François Baby for the maintenance of Tug steamers below Quebec from the commencement of the contract to the present date; the amount paid in each year as direct aid under Mr. Baby's contract; the amount paid in each year from the Public Funds in reduction of rates charged to ship owners, and ALSO the amount advanced by Government towards the building of Mr. Baby's steamers."

In the first year of his contract, 1854, Baby received approximately £8,000 for "tug services" from the provincial coffers. This was increased in the years 1855–1858 to £11,300 per annum. During this same period and until the termination of his contract, the government also advanced more than £200,000 in payments for the new steam tugs. These would have included the new steamers *Queen Victoria*, *Napoleon III*, and *Lady Head*, all built on the Clyde by Robert Napier, who presumably had agreed to accept payment for these vessels during the term of Baby's contract for tug services.

The public accounts also reveal that during the contract, Baby was reimbursed by government for vessels towed at the advertised 50 per cent reduction to the tune of an additional 30 per cent, calculated on the full fare. Statistics also noted the number of vessels towed in 1857 totalled 104 when tows averaged from £11 to £58. The following year, there was a marked decrease in tows—down to only 31, but the cost of tows had increased dramatically, averaging £84–£259. By 1859 that latter figure had increased again to £320, giving some credence to the criticism levelled by the shipping owners over excessive rates.

François Baby had mixed success in business but left his mark on the St. Lawrence. He now chose to move on to pursue yet another career—this time in politics. In June 1861, running as a Conservative, he was elected to the legislative assembly for the division of Stadacona (Quebec City). He went on to hold this position for the rest of his life, which proved not to be long. He died quietly of heart disease at his home on St. Louis Street on August 6, 1864, at the age of sixty-nine.

The Quebec papers mourned the death of this man "whose liberal character and generous heart will forever be missed by his circle of friends." That circle included the political elite in Quebec; his pallbearers on the August 10 funeral included Sir E. P. Taché, Hon. George E. Cartier, Joseph-Noel Bossé, George Pemberton, and Justices René-Édouard Caron and Jean-Thomas Taschereau.

The 1860 season on the St. Lawrence began for *Queen Victoria* with little fanfare. She went about her now accustomed duties in government service supplying lighthouses and engaging in towage whenever called upon. That summer, however, an event for which her namesake, Her Majesty Queen Victoria, was responsible took place that forever altered her use and reputation as a tug steamer. Henceforth, she could no longer be described as simply a tug but rather she graduated to a royal yacht.

During the previous five years, Montreal, just upriver from Quebec City, had been the scene of the largest and most challenging engineering feat ever undertaken in British North America. Work had just concluded on the construction of a bridge, the first to span the mighty St. Lawrence River. This was no ordinary bridge, and this was no ordinary river. Built as a tubular bridge, the original deck was a long structural metal tube made of prefabricated wrought-iron sections manufactured in England and shipped to site. At the height of the construction, some three hundred men were employed in the work which was completed at a cost approaching $7 million.

This marvel of the industrial world focused international attention on the united Provinces of Canada and Premier George Cartier felt it worthy of a grand opening. On May 4, 1859, as construction neared an end, Cartier wrote to Queen Victoria on behalf of the Legislative Council

Opening of Victoria Bridge in Montreal, 1860.

of the Province of Canada, formally requesting she open the Victoria Bridge in Montreal, which he described as "the most gigantic work of modern days."

She declined. In the written response, Cartier was told that "Her Majesty feels that her duties at the seat of the Empire prevent so long an absence and at so great a distance as a visit to Canada would necessarily require." It was not a total rebuke, as her scribe went on to say:

> *The Queen commands me to express Her hope that when the time for the opening of the bridge is fixed, it may be possible for His Royal Highness the Prince of Wales to attend the ceremony in Her Majesty's name and to witness these gratifying scenes in which the Queen is herself unable to participate. The Queen trusts that nothing may interfere with this arrangement for it is Her Majesty's sincere desire that the young Prince, on whom the Crown of this Empire will devolve may have the opportunity of visiting that portion of Her Dominions from which this address has proceeded, and may become acquainted with a people in whose rapid progress towards greatness Her Majesty, in common with her subjects in Great Britain feels a lively and enduring sympathy.*

No one could accuse the Queen's secretary of being short on words! The die was now cast and preparations began in earnest for the first royal visit to North America by an heir to the British throne. It would be the first of many such visits, which to this very day continue to excite and capture Canadians' monarchal spirit.

Not to be outdone, when President James Buchanan heard of the plans for the prince to visit British North America, he promptly wrote the queen with an invitation to have the prince extend his tour to the United States, including a personal invitation to the White House. Queen Victoria agreed on her son's behalf. And so similar preparations began south of the border.

Apparently Queen Victoria's decision to decline Cartier's invitation was not entirely due the pressing business of running the Empire. In fact, she and her eldest son, Albert Edward, did not get along. She considered him somewhat of a playboy and blamed him for the death of her husband, Albert, which she felt may have been hastened due to the stresses brought on by this son's frivolous antics. Sending him off to North America would give her some relief from his presence for an extended period of time.

On July 9, 1860, the Prince of Wales, just eighteen years of age, boarded the royal yacht *Victoria and Albert*, which transported him to Plymouth, where she met up with the Channel squadron comprised of various British naval vessels. There he joined HMS *Hero*, which together with HMS *Ariadne*, set sail for Newfoundland. A third warship, HMS *Flying Fish*, with Commander Hope had left earlier to be in Newfoundland to greet the prince upon his arrival there. The crossing on *Hero* produced some excitement as, for several days on the voyage, she resorted to a tow by *Ariadne* "being short of fuel." This may explain why it took thirteen days to reach the safety of St. John's Harbour, where she was met by thousands of enthralled Newfoundlanders. The stay there was brief but memorable. Upon departure the "inhabitants of Newfoundland" presented the prince with a real Newfoundland dog, appropriately named Cabot, after the celebrated explorer Sebastian Cabot. The dog would be a companion to the prince throughout the remainder of the sea voyage.

Departing St. John's, the royal convoy made an unscheduled stop in Sydney, Cape Breton, before arriving in Halifax on July 30. There, as was the case in Newfoundland, Nova Scotians went out of their way to fete the royal visitor. The prince's maritime tour continued to neighbouring New Brunswick where he was entertained in Saint John and Fredericton

HMS Hero

before returning to Nova Scotia. At the town of Pictou the prince once again boarded HMS *Hero* and set course for Charlottetown, Prince Edward Island. Rain had plagued the prince during his tour, to a point where he had jokingly been described by local media as "the raining Prince." Prince Edward Island weather was no different, although the rains there did nothing to dampen the spirits of the welcoming public on that small colonial island.

The Prince of Wales had now experienced the Maritime provinces and Newfoundland, where he had been received with unabashed affection of his loyal subjects. Now it was westward, across the Gulf of St. Lawrence to Gaspé, where for the first time the prince would lay his eyes upon Canada.

On the evening of August 12 the Prince of Wales aboard HMS *Hero*, accompanied by HMS *Ariadne* and HMS *Flying Fish*, arrived at Gaspé. It was sunset, with "the reds and yellows of the sky contrasting beautifully with the indistinct greens of the shore and the hazy blues of the distant hills"—in the words of a professional writer accompanying the entourage on the tour.

The Canadian government steamers *Queen Victoria* and *Lady Head* were already there. On-board *Queen Victoria* was Sir Edmund Walker Head, Governor General of British North America, and the ministry of Canada, all of whom had come down from Quebec on the provincial steamer to welcome the prince to Canada. *Queen Victoria* gallantly met and dipped her ensigns to the prince's fleet, following which all five vessels dropped their anchors in the land-locked harbour. Once secure, HMS *Hero* hailed *Queen Victoria*, asking if the Governor General was aboard. *Queen Victoria* replied, "He's on board." That was the extent of communication as those aboard each ship settled in for the night.

The next morning, the thirteenth, at 8:30 A.M. Governor General Head and one of his aides left *Queen Victoria* and went on-board *Hero*, where they were received by a salute, by a guard of honour of the Royal Marines, and by the prince and his suite. A deputation of Crown officials from the Gaspé District arrived from shore in several boats and once aboard, presented the prince with a petition for him to allow Gaspé to be called Port Albert in commemoration of the visit. The prince, demonstrating utter discretion, gently declined, expressing his regret to be unable to comply with their request, as it was a matter for provincial authorities. And so the region retains its name as Gaspé.

Shortly afterwards the Canadian ministry proceeded on-board HMS *Hero* and were presented to the prince by the Duke of Newcastle. Some of the significant names among the ministers of the Province of Canada were Hon. George E. Cartier and John A. Macdonald, attorneys general for Canada East and Canada West; A. T. Galt, minister of finance; John Ross, president of the Executive Council and minister of agriculture; and John Rose, commissioner of public works. After lunching with the prince, they returned to the *Queen Victoria* along with Governor General Head and weighed anchor for the Saguenay.

The Saguenay River is located approximately halfway up the north shore of the St. Lawrence River towards Quebec City. Its tidal waters run inland about sixty miles to Chicoutimi. It is steeped in history. Tadoussac, located at the mouth of the river, was founded as a French colonial trading post as far back as 1600. In recent years, the Saguenay has become a popular destination for cruise ships. One of the pioneers of Saguenay cruising was the paddle steamship *Unicorn*, which carried the mail for Cunard Line between Pictou, Nova Scotia, and Quebec City. When time and circumstance permitted, she transported government officials and other dignitaries for excursions to the Saguenay in the 1840s.

The provincial steamers *Queen Victoria* and *Lady Head* had led the way up to the Saguenay and were on site when HMS *Hero* arrived with the Prince of Wales. *Hero* had taken up a local pilot from the south side of the St. Lawrence while en route, and in an embarrassing incident, the same pilot managed to ground the flagship upon a reef at the mouth of the river. *Hero* remained fetched up there for three hours before getting off without serious injury. The delay frustrated plans ashore that had been carefully made by the inhabitants of Saguenay and Grand Bay—and very likely later brought the luckless pilot to the attention of his masters at Trinity House of Quebec for reprimand.

Upon witnessing the *Hero* incident, the fleet was deterred from entering the Saguenay and judiciously chose to remain at anchor outside the river mouth. The prince and suite joined Governor General Head and his party aboard *Queen Victoria* and proceeded up the Saguenay. While steaming upriver there were numerous cannon salutes, which Captain Paul Pouliot, master of *Queen Victoria*, promptly acknowledged.

According to a correspondent's report of the excursion, "The day was very showery and cold and the 'tourists' suited themselves to the exigencies of the weather, the Prince wearing a pot hat and the roughest of clothes, the Governor General, the Ministers and the rest of the Party wearing waterproofs of some kind. The *Victoria* went 45 miles up the river past Cape Eternity and, as the weather was unpropitious, her passengers sought consolation in cigars and refreshments. They all admired the scenery exceedingly and perhaps the rain and clouds added much to its usual wildness and grandeur."

The weather also produced a strong headwind and ebb current. The weather in combination with the late start occasioned by *Hero*'s grounding rendered it impossible to reach Grand Bay, where the civic reception was unavoidably cancelled, much to the chagrin of the local populace. The return trip downriver was made at speed. As darkness fell, *Queen Victoria* anchored alongside *Hero*. The prince and his suite took up their familiar quarters again for the night.

The next morning dawned bright. Following an early breakfast, the prince again came aboard *Queen Victoria* and joined his shipmate hosts from the previous day. It was an impressive assemblage of politicians, military and civilian passengers that included Their Excellencies Sir Edmund Head and the Earl of Mulgrave, the Duke of Newcastle, Major General Bruce, Commodore Seymour, Dr. Auckland, Captain Grey, Major Teasdale, Mr. Engleheart, Mr. Ellis, Mr. Stapleton, Captain Retallack, and Messrs. MacDonald, Cartier, Galt, Morrison, Ross, Smith, and Morin.

Adding to this number was the Prince of Wales and his suite, all of which must have challenged the diplomatic and social skills of Captain Pouliot, his officers and crew of *Queen Victoria*.

With everyone safely onboard, the steamer now in service as a royal yacht, proceeded upriver about fifteen miles to the Sainte-Marguerite River, where local Indigenous peoples had set up a campsite, complete with tents from which the royal party would try their hands at salmon fishing.

Not many salmon were caught; perhaps they were frightened off by cannon fire. The consort vessel *Flying Fish* chose this day to go up the Saguenay and take with it the greater part of the squadron officers. While passing by the "Royal tent encampment" where the Royal Standard and Union Jack flags fluttered, a royal salute of twenty-one guns was fired from *Flying Fish*, with the result, "the echoes among the precipitous rocks close at hand and the echoes from the more distant hills were strikingly sublime and much delighted the royal party."

Any disappointment in the fishing was more than compensated for by the adventure in ascending and descending the Sainte-Marguerite River in a slew of birchbark canoes. The trip upriver took "three toilsome hours," but the return down through the rapids with the prince in the lead canoe, which flew a miniature standard in the bow, was accomplished in a mere forty minutes. It was quite a rush for the entire troupe, which thereafter returned to the flotilla. The next day they made their way up the St. Lawrence to Quebec City.

The public accounts would later reveal costs of $2,550 associated with the visit and excursion of HRM Prince of Wales aboard *Queen Victoria*, a princely sum for that time.

Before concluding his tour of Canada, the Prince of Wales had two other functions to perform. The first was the original reason for the Queen's invitation to Canada—the ceremonial opening of the new Victoria Bridge at Montreal on August 25, 1860. The bridge was decked out for the occasion and ready for the prince to lay the last piece of masonry: "On the platform which was covered with scarlet cloth the Prince was met by Mr. Hodges, the builder who, as soon as the royal party were grouped around, handed the Prince a silver trowel wherewith to spread the mortar. HRH did this in a workmanlike manner and then the stone which hung suspended from a derrick and measured 10.5' by 2' by 3'4" was gently lowered to its resting place. The prince then gave three taps with a mallet and this part of the ceremony was complete."

One further function remained before the bridge was officially opened. "The Prince then descended and took his seat along with a numerous body of officials in a beautiful (train) car built specially for the purpose, open all around the roof, supported simply by wooden pillars. The engine screamed and the party were driven to the centre of the two mile tube where they got out and the prince placed the last rivet of the bridge in its place which was at once hammered in by a chosen body of mechanics. Then they got aboard again and went completely through the tube and returned to a luncheon in the great car shed at Point St. Charles." The Victoria Bridge was now officially open. His Royal Highness crossed it by train a few days later, on August 30, en route to Ottawa, the new capital of Canada, where he had one more task to perform.

There is some truth to the suggestion that a painting was responsible for the choice of Ottawa as the site for Canada's capital. Lady Anna Head at some point had painted a landscape of the Ottawa River, which she presented to Queen Victoria. The Queen had been asked in 1857 to select a permanent capital. She was suitably impressed with what she perceived was an idyllic setting as painted, and in 1858 chose the site—Barrack Hill in the lumber town of Ottawa, until recently called Bytown, over the more established cities of Toronto, Quebec City, Kingston, and Montreal—as the new capital of Canada.

Construction had begun on the Parliament Buildings in 1859, but now a formal ceremony for laying a cornerstone was required to dedicate this important undertaking. An account of that event offers a sense of its importance: "On September 1, 1860, at 11 A.M. His Royal [H]ighness the Prince of Wales left the new hotel where he was staying and which, in honour of Her Majesty's choice of Ottawa for the seat of government is called Victoria House, and proceeded to lay the foundation stone of the Parliament Buildings. The day was fine and the scene consequently, magnificent. A large crowd in the thousands was present."

After the chaplain to the legislative council opened with a prayer, the prince and chief members of the suite advanced to the stone of beautiful white Canadian marble or crystalized limestone, brought from Portage-du-Fort. On it was the simple inscription: "This cornerstone of the building intended to receive the Legislature of Canada was laid by Albert Edward, Prince of Wales on the 1st day of September, 1860."

A glass-bottle time capsule was place in a cavity in the stone. The piece of parchment in it contained the names of the members of the legislative assembly, the members of the government of Canada, and other officials for the occasion. In a final regal touch, the work was tested by the use of a stonemason's level, which was supported by a lion and a unicorn. Collectively, these heraldic figures are symbols of the United Kingdom, the lion representing England and the unicorn, Scotland. They are integral features of both the royal coat of arms for the United Kingdom as well as for Canada. (The arms featuring both the lion and the unicorn are embossed on Canadian passports.)

As the Prince of Wales departed British North America to continue his royal tour in the United States, the steamer *Queen Victoria* returned to her normal service on the St. Lawrence. No longer was she a mere tug tender. She had for a time assumed the mantle of a royal yacht and had performed the service admirably. She would soon be called upon to reprise the role.

For now, Captain Paul Pouliot would resume his more familiar work as master of a provincial steamer, taking tows and supplying lights in the St. Lawrence River and Gulf of St. Lawrence. He would not soon forget the royal tour of 1860 and the friendship that ensued between himself as captain of *Queen Victoria* and his royal guest the Prince of Wales. As evidence of that friendship the prince had presented Pouliot with a small compass and pen set, which would remain a treasured memento of that occasion.

On November 2, 1861, Viscount Charles Stanley Monck replaced Sir Edmund Walker Head as Governor General of British North America. For the next seven years he would play a significant role in the emergence of a new nation in Canada's first Governor General post on July 1, 1867, and as the last Governor General of the Province of Canada.

On July 27, 1864, Captain Pouliot was once again called upon to offer his steamer as an imperial launch. His Excellency Governor General Monck and suite boarded *Queen Victoria* at Quebec City for a cruise of the Saguenay and various other ports of call on the St. Lawrence River. It was largely a fishing expedition and family outing, as included were a number of Monck family members. Among them were his brother Richard Monck and his wife, Frances, whose diary contains interesting insights into the trip.

On departure the *Queen Victoria* "was covered with flags and looked very gay." The entourage occupied much of the passenger accommodation. Typical of that era, there were both ladies' and gentlemen's cabins with reportedly hard beds. After spending the first night at Rivière-du-Loup, *Queen Victoria* set off the following day for the mouth of the Saguenay, where most of the party went ashore to fish in the pouring rain. At day's end they steamed back about three miles to the village of Tadoussac and anchored for the night.

The *Queen Victoria* steamed to Laval Bay the next morning. From there some in the party set off in canoes to fish the Laval River. Frances Monck spent more time on-board *Queen Victoria* than on shore. Consequently, she struck up a convivial relationship with Captain Paul Pouliot; "pronounced Pouillote—we all like him," she wrote in her diary. The captain had plenty of time for his passengers, often reassuring them about the weather and not to fear the thunder and lightning, which marred part of their trip. Frances wrote: "He was very kind to me about thunder and said there would be very little. The rain came down in torrents....I was afraid of the rain and the darkness, but the captain reassured me." He looked out for their safety while on-board and at one point very discreetly discouraged some of his passengers from leaving the steamer, fearing the difficulty of landing on "this unknown shore." Captain Pouliot told Frances Monk about his experience with the Prince of Wales during his trip to the Saguenay just a few years earlier. He shared with her an account of how the prince had given him a pencil case in the shape of a telescope and a compass in the shape of a cocked hat as ornaments for his chain.

On the trip, the *Queen Victoria* went up the Saguenay to see Cap Éternité and Cap Trinité before returning to Tadoussac via Sainte-Marguerite River. The fishing proved to be much better than what the Prince of Wales had experienced. Governor General Monck and his fishing friends caught 162 trout in one day. While at Tadoussac, the voyagers were enchanted by the spectacle of the northern lights, which Captain Pouliot told them was supposed to be the reflection of the sun shining on the ice at the North Pole.

The ladies in particular seemed to enjoy the company of the crew on *Queen Victoria*. In an interesting aside Frances Monck wrote: "There was a handsome man onboard, the second mate called Domonique Beaulieu, very Spanish looking, and so civil and good-humoured, we all loved him!"

Captain Pouliot evidently had some family of his own. Mrs. Monck observed that he took advantage of the once-in-a-lifetime opportunity to share these special occasions with his son. In her diary she noted: "The captain had his little boy on board and he told Miss Frend he brought him because he might never see a Lord again and that he said to his boy that he ought to be proud to be in the company of so many titled people. He also brought him on board when the Prince was there (1860) because he thought he would never see a Prince again!"

By August 3, the *Queen Victoria* had returned to Quebec City, following a most successful outing on the Saguenay. The gentlemen were sad to be back home and ashore again. Most of the ladies, however, were happy to return to "large bedrooms, with space to turn round, instead of little cramped-up cabins and rocky beds where you could not move without hitting yourself."

As for Captain Pouliot, it was just a matter of readjusting to routine once again. Fate was of another mind. Within a few short weeks, *Queen Victoria* would embark on a grand voyage, one never contemplated when she was conceived, and which would ultimately define her historic role in the birth of the new nation of Canada.

Part 2

The Canadian Confederate Cruiser: Steaming Towards a New Nation

CHAPTER 4

Not Yet a Nation: Maritime Union or Confederation?

Politics in Canada have always been dominated by language—French and English, reflecting the historical struggle between France and Britain for supremacy over what was initially colonized as New France and subsequently became British North America. As history reveals, the French were the first Europeans to discover and settle. The French explorer and colonizer Pierre Dugua de Mons, accompanied by Samuel de Champlain, founded the first permanent French settlement in Canada at Port-Royal in 1605. Shortly after, in 1608, Champlain founded Quebec on the site of the former Iroquois settlement at Stadacona, where he served as administrator for the rest of his life, thus earning the title Father of New France.

So it was that the French became well-established in the upper St. Lawrence region in the early seventeenth century. Colonization from France, while initially sporadic, picked up considerably under the administration of Jean Talon, intendant of New France. He was tasked with building up the population. During Champlain's time and until his death in 1835, males had predominated, but if stability was to be achieved, it was essential that every settler should have a wife and rear a family. Historian Gerald S. Graham in his book titled *A Concise History of Canada*, helps to account for what led to a dramatic increase in population:

> Marriage became therefore a matter not of inclination, but of duty. The bachelor received no sympathy from government, and "single blessedness" was soon the subject of heavy penalties. Talon arranged for the shipment (from France) of potential brides, and on their arrival reluctant males were given fifteen days to conduct courtship and seal a partnership. In these circumstances, it is understandable that a certain amount of scrimmaging occurred at the docks. Occasionally the ships brought dubious characters who were promptly returned to France, but most of the immigrants were "demoiselles bien choisies," of good health and good will, a

> mixture of middle class and peasant stock, capable apparently of standing comparison in charm and sturdiness with the original "jolies brunettes canadiennes" already acclimatized to pioneer life.

French dominance in British North America was further strengthened by the broad-based network of feudal land tenures and feudal service known as the seigneurial system, which was introduced from France. The land grants or seigneuries were most prevalent along the shores of the St. Lawrence and Richelieu Rivers. Grants were usually long and narrow strips, from fifty to several hundred acres, with waterfronts of three to seven miles. In pledge of fealty to the king, an undertaking to perform military service and to clear and cultivate the land in a timely fashion, the seigneur was given the land. He then sublet to tenants or habitants who had complete security of possession, as long as they paid a nominal rent and carried out the tasks required of pioneer farmers.

Most of the dwellings of both seigneurs and habitants were constructed along the riverbanks, in time creating parishes, centred around the Catholic church. Parochial associations soon began to take shape around the church, and over time it was the parish priest, the *curé* and not the seigneur who became the friend, counsellor, and protector of the habitant. It is an ironclad bond still prevalent to this day.

This old-style French feudal system prevailed, became entrenched, and by the late eighteenth century the colony of Quebec was inhabited by an overwhelming preponderance of French-speaking subjects of the Crown. About that time, the American War of Independence gave rise to a massive exodus of United Empire Loyalists to the Maritime provinces as well as to the western part of Quebec around Lake Erie and Lake Ontario. These Loyalist settlers had grown up in an atmosphere of political freedom and upon arrival were not long in pushing their rights to enjoy British civil law and representative government. This movement soon succeeded, and in 1791 the Constitutional Act divided the colony of Quebec into two colonies, Upper and Lower Canada, or what became the provinces of Ontario (English-speaking) and Quebec (French-speaking).

This political division remained the case for almost fifty years, when in 1840 the Act of Union brought Lower and Upper Canada together to form the united Province of Canada. By this time, however, a half-century of segregation and self-government had established its course. French Canada would prove to be too firmly entrenched to ever be seriously threatened as a distinct culture in a future Canadian nation: shades of Hugh MacLennan's classic novel *Two Solitudes*.

The cultural divide persevered in the Province of Canada, which took the form of Canada West and Canada East. The province was expansive, stretching one thousand miles from Gaspé to Sarnia and united by a common geography that included the St. Lawrence, its estuary, river, and the Great Lakes hinterland. However, Canada East, the future Quebec, retained its language, civil law, and educational institutions, all closely tied to the Catholic church, and distinct from the language, law, and education in Canada West, the future Ontario.

Not surprisingly, the Province of Canada proved to be very difficult to govern. In the years following union, the two regions pulled against each other more and more. As one Ontario newspaper described it, "Here are two provinces of different nationalities...and to a great extent of different customs; these two provinces are professedly united, when in reality they are at variance, and to all appearances there is no prospect of their ever acting in unison."

The years had produced a succession of failed coalition governments, which by 1864 had ended in political gridlock. The leading Canadian politicians of the day on both sides of the divided house were at their wits' end. A heroic remedy to bring about a strong and lasting government was required. Eyes were cast east to the Maritime provinces for a resolution, which by this time the Canadian politicians had concluded might best lie in a united federation of all the provinces of British North America. At this time, British North America was made up of Prince Edward Island, New Brunswick, and Nova Scotia (collectively referred to as the Maritime provinces), Province of Canada, British Columbia, Vancouver Island, and Newfoundland.

Political historians agree that, for Canada, at this time in history, change was essential. Unification of Upper and Lower Canada had not brought about the desired results, and by 1864 politicians of all political stripes in the united province were committed to change. For them, maintaining the status quo was not an option—they were driven to change to the political framework within which they toiled, and in the process, to better their own standing and prospects within that framework.

This objective was not at all the case in the four eastern colonies of Nova Scotia, Prince Edward Island, New Brunswick, and Newfoundland.

However, the concept of a confederation was not new. It had arisen in the assemblies of the various provinces from time to time but was never debated with any degree of enthusiasm. It was often a favourite subject with after-dinner speakers and restless politicians, but for all practical purposes, a political abstraction. It remained "a glittering ideal that few cared to transform into the dross of everyday reality." A Toronto newspaper correspondent writing from Halifax in 1864 observed, "There has not been in these provinces a tithe of the political agitation which has distracted Canada.…The people here are rather content to suffer the evils they bear than fly to others they know not of." And so life went on in the Maritimes with little heed paid to the growing agitation in Canada.

Instead, each of the provinces outside of Canada retained their own government and independence, which they continued to enjoy in stark contrast to the disdain they held for the political quagmire in Canada. Whenever the subject of confederation arose, politicians in the Maritimes turned to thoughts of another arrangement that better suited their needs and purposes—Maritime Union. Despite pressure, particularly from successive governors in New Brunswick, public support was negligible and public enthusiasm non-existent.

The prospects for a Maritime Union flickered to life in the spring of 1864, as a result of what Nova Scotians and New Brunswickers perceived as Canadian deception arising from failed Intercolonial Railway negotiations. The Maritime provinces had lobbied hard with Canada to complete the railway between Rivière-du-Loup and Truro. Nova Scotia had gone so far as to agree upon a cost-sharing formula with Canada and New Brunswick. When the negotiations failed, recriminations in the Maritimes were swift. The movement developed sufficient momentum that in the spring sessions of 1864 all three legislatures of the Maritimes proposed resolutions authorizing the appointment of delegates to a conference on Maritime Union.

No sooner had the notion caught fire, than the flame of Maritime Union flickered, largely as a result of timely manoeuvring by Canadian politicians. In an apparent effort to keep the Intercolonial project alive, Canada had decided to proceed immediately with a survey of the line. This was not the same thing as an agreement to build the line, but it had the desired effect of causing pause. Skeptics doubted the value of a gesture that came from so unstable a government, but just the same, the proffered Canadian survey weakened the impetus towards Maritime Union just at the time when it ought to have been at its most vigorous.

In Prince Edward Island, residents were reluctant to consider any kind of union, fearing they might have to abandon their legislature, which they held so dear. Their position was succinctly put by Premier J. H. Gray, who said, "I would not allow myself or my country to be swamped by any body of men on earth. We, Sir, are here to maintain our rights and we shall never enter a Union which will deprive us of this birthright." Even Leader of the Opposition George Coles could not disagree. He put it more bluntly, describing the argument for Maritime Union as "a piece of political clap-trap."

However, mere courtesy demanded a reply to the invitation of delegates for the conference on Maritime Union. Not wishing to miss out on issues that might be of importance, the Prince Edward Island assembly passed a form of restricted resolution that authorized the appointment of five delegates to confer, not on Maritime Union, but rather on the expediency of it. The resolution gave no authority for any real negotiations.

The *Acadian Recorder* newspaper in Nova Scotia appears to have voiced the strongest support for the proposition of Maritime Union. An article suggested that Maritime Union should not resemble the unfortunate Canadian experiment: "We hope our public men will manage to annihilate all distinctions on the Colonial map and on the colonial brain. If we are to join together, let us be one people in reality. Let the name Acadia absorb forever the names of New Brunswick, Nova Scotia, and Prince Edward Island. Let there be no Upper and Lower, East and West, or North and South with us."

There were two other major factors at play during the period 1860–1864, and both were to influence decision makers as they pondered the weighty subjects of Maritime Union and Confederation. To the south, the United States had a union matter of its own. The controversy over slavery could not be resolved with diplomacy. The result was the American Civil War, which began when southern forces of the eleven Confederate States attacked the northern Union Army at Fort Sumter in April 1861. The war would rage on for the next three years until the North prevailed and the Confederates surrendered in the spring of 1864. But not before deaths on both sides, North and South, approximated a staggering 750,000.

The other issue, related to the American conflict, was Great Britain's indifference towards the colonial empire in British North America. Britain had begun to look at opportunities for relinquishing her hold to relieve the ongoing expense of maintaining the colonies, particularly potential defence costs in the face of an increasingly bellicose northern United States.

So by the summer of 1864, there was a certain unease permeating the Maritime provinces, all brought about by external forces beyond their control. They didn't know it then, but politicians in Nova Scotia, Prince Edward Island, New Brunswick, and to a lesser extent Newfoundland, were about to be assailed by their political counterparts in Canada in a concerted, timely, well-orchestrated, and united pitch for confederation of all the provinces of British North America.

These external circumstances played directly into the hands of the Canadian politicians, and they were quick to take advantage. They immediately saw a golden opportunity to broach the confederation subject with their Maritime counterparts in an effort to extricate themselves from their own political muddle. In a bizarre turn of events, the Canadians arranged through Governor General Monck to invite themselves to a conference ostensibly on Maritime Union, which had not yet been arranged, for the sole purpose of persuading the Maritime premiers of the merits of confederation. The "offer for an invitation" was accepted (Maritimers have always been known for their hospitality), and between Lieutenant-Governor Richard Graves MacDonnell of Nova Scotia and Lieutenant-Governor George Dundas of Prince Edward Island, Charlottetown was fixed as the place for the conference scheduled for September 1.

In the few short weeks left before the conference, there was a brief revival of interest in the subject of Maritime Union. After all, this was what the conference was set up to consider. Significantly, and in sharp contrast to the Canadian ministry, there was no unanimity among the three Maritime provinces on the subject. Nor was there any attempt to meet among themselves to plan for the conference. Putting forth a united front was wishful thinking—each province had their own take on the subject based on self-interest and political expediency.

Newfoundland had to this point not been part of the discussion around union. At the very last moment, the colony was invited to attend at Charlottetown. The response came that notice was too short and timing inconvenient, with a recent change in governors. One thing was a sure bet: having secured an invitation to attend, the Canadian ministry wasted no time in formulating detailed plans for their assault on Charlottetown.

As the summer of 1864 wore on, politicians in the Maritimes continued with their daily routines. Although they had no political appetite for the subject of confederation, they would lend an ear to what the Canadian ministry might have to say in Charlottetown. They would host a conference on Maritime Union, another concept which lacked any broad support or any real excitement in the Maritime provinces. The eastern colonies, comfortable in their own political realms, were ripe for attack. The first wave came in the form of a great "getting-to-know-you party" at the invitation of the Maritime provinces.

Call it fate, stroke of good luck, or pure happenstance, no student of history can underestimate the importance to the evolution of Confederation, which may be attributed to the events that transpired in Halifax and Saint John just a few weeks before the Charlottetown Conference. The background was simple: Canadians and Maritimers were strangers to each other. Geographically Canada was a world apart from the Maritime provinces. The political players in Canada had, for the most part, never met those in the Maritimes. Maritimers (even then) were suspicious of the Canadians, who they quietly regarded as untrustworthy, irresponsible, and incapable of running their own union. From the Maritimers' perspective Canadians were "all too often bent on relieving themselves of their embarrassments at the expense of others." The remedy for this significant impasse was, in the minds of two Canadians—Sir Sandford Fleming and Thomas D'Arcy McGee—to get acquainted in person.

The wheels for such an eventuality had been put in motion a year earlier, when both McGee and Fleming had visited Halifax. In April of 1864, upon a return visit to Halifax, Fleming approached Premier Charles Tupper with a suggestion that Nova Scotia host a visit from the Canadians. In short order, after Saint John took up this initiative, invitations were extended to Canadians to visit both New Brunswick and Nova Scotia that summer. The fact that the Confederation proposal was in the air around this time made the invitation all the more attractive to Canadians, who were only too quick to accept. In the end, approximately one hundred Canadians, including eighteen members of the Canadian legislative council and thirty-two from the assembly, representatives of twenty-three newspapers, as well as prominent Canadian businessmen, descended upon Halifax and Saint John.

The Canadian contingent arrived first at Saint John by steamer via Portland, Maine. The reception upon their arrival was unbelievable: as many as fifteen thousand townspeople crowded the waterfront to greet the visitors. During a five-day visit in New Brunswick the Canadians were feted with dinners, speeches, and an outpouring of good will in their travels between Saint John and Fredericton. French Canadians who made up more than a quarter of the Canadian contingent were encouraged and responded happily in singing French Canadian songs and other old paddling songs, "swinging imaginary paddles from side to side of invisible canoes as they sang." Their enthusiasm was infectious, and their hosts got caught up in it. So much so, one of the newspaper correspondents reported that "Maritimers will labour under the impression that French is the universal language in Canada and that French songs are as familiar to all Canadians as John Brown's soul."

On August 10 the Canadians crossed the Bay of Fundy by the steamer *Emperor* to Windsor, where they were met by Tupper, Annand, and Howe, who accompanied them by coach to Halifax. The following few days were to witness fervent, almost infantile, expressions of bonhomie on the part of the Maritime hosts towards their Canadian guests.

Soon after arriving in the city, the visitors were invited to partake in the annual Hodge-Podge and Chowder Party as guests of the Royal Halifax Yacht Club, known today as the Royal Nova Scotia Yacht Squadron. August 12 began with a sail around the harbour and a rendezvous at Prince's Lodge, in Bedford Basin, on the grounds of the Duke of Kent's home during his posting in Halifax years before. Here the participants picnicked in grand style, and throughout the afternoon engaged in "manly and exhilarating games," quite the antithesis of Victorian gentlemen.

This of course was reported in considerable detail by some of the travelling correspondents. The *Toronto Leader* gave a colourful account of the scene at Prince's Lodge: "Leap-frog at once became the order of the day and a lively scene ensued. Members of the Upper House backed members of the Lower House with an agility that was wonderful. Bluenoses sprang over Canadians with a shriek of delight. Canadians bounded over New Brunswickers and tripped over Nova Scotians. Editors and correspondents mingled in the fray and periled their valuable persons by seeking the bubble reputation."

It must have been a lively scene. Speeches followed the frolic, aided and abetted by an abundance of wine from orators speaking on behalf of both hosts and visitors, Joseph Howe for the Maritimers and D'Arcy McGee for the Canadians. If this wasn't enough to stir the soul and senses, the crowd was roiled by the sound of bagpipes, with several adept Scotsmen among the group feeling duty-bound to perform the Highland fling. The star of the show was the "nimble old Mayor of Fredericton who is said to have danced the friskiest carle of them all."

A subsequent report of the Prince's Lodge picnic in the *Halifax Morning Sun* took a more lenient view of that event and admonished "some malicious persons who have circulated a report that the Picnic of the Yacht Club was a scene of riot and drunkenness." To this suggestion the paper responded, "Having been present from first to last, we can testify that a greater slander was never uttered. Of fun and frolic—of hearty song-singing—somewhat noisy withal—such as Frenchmen love—there was plenty; but of riot or excess in eating or drinking we observed none. We never saw a more sober or better conducted party anywhere."

Joseph Howe was at his loquacious best in entertaining his new-found Canadian friends with a speech at a dinner in Halifax on August 13. Some of his remarks, while very well received by his guests, would later come back to haunt him. Even Howe could be caught up in the sublime atmosphere and good feeling brought on by food and drink. On this occasion he reportedly said, "He [Howe] was not one of those who thanked God that he was a Nova Scotian merely, for he was a Canadian as well. He had never thought he was a Nova Scotian, but looked across the broad continent...and studied the mode by which it would be consolidated...and why should union not be brought about? Was it because we wished to live and die in our insignificance?"

In these and the years that followed, political historians and students of our political history might well be excused for any uncertainty they felt about Joseph Howe's views on confederation. Depending on the occasion—and the speech—he was at once a proponent of Maritime Union, an Imperialist who advocated a broader, more meaningful relationship between the colony of Nova Scotia and the British Empire, and a staunch anti-confederate known to advance the cause of political union with Canada.

Joseph Howe took full advantage of the few remaining opportunities to fraternize with the Canadian and New Brunswick visitors. On a beautiful August 15, the vice admiral invited the visitors aboard the war steamer *Lily* for an excursion out Halifax Harbour to Sambro Light, then up Bedford Basin, and back between 11:00 A.M. and 6:00 P.M. Halifax newspapers captured the tour: During the cruise, the flagship's band "discoursed sweet music" and "the feast of good things provided was disposed of—the dread of sea-sickness over-coming but a few—and dancing was engaged so far as space provided." The common sentiment was that "the hours spent in this very delightful trip will doubtless be long remembered."

The party was nearing an end, but not before the Honourable T. D. McGee took the platform one more time to preach upon his favourite topic: Confederation. The venue for his parting speech was the Temperance Hall, and he did not disappoint. There is little doubt that by now a strong friendship had emerged between Howe and McGee, based on the respect each had for the passion and oratorical skills of the other. Howe was quoted as saying that McGee was particularly eloquent over a bottle of wine. Whether he was so influenced on this occasion may be left to speculation, but clearly the Halifax press was swayed by McGee's speech on confederation. The next day the *Halifax Morning Chronicle* reported, "In all that assembly there was scarcely one, and, no matter how prejudiced or opposed before, who was not convinced by the burning eloquence of this modern Demosthenos."

McGee's speech was a fitting end to the week. The next day, as the visitors departed for home, Joseph Howe boarded HMS *Lily* once again, this time as fisheries commissioner on official business to Newfoundland. Howe, along with Messrs. Tupper, Henry, Dickie, and Archibald, had just been designated Nova Scotian delegates to the conference at Charlottetown on the subject of union of the colonies. Howe had sought leave from his duties as fisheries commissioner to attend, but was refused by the colonial secretary. One can only wonder what, if any, difference his participation may have made in the outcome of the Charlottetown meetings.

The Canadians' visit to New Brunswick and Nova Scotia was both timely and fortuitous for the confederate cause. While public sentiment in neither New Brunswick nor Nova Scotia overtly supported federal union—and the Canadian press was fair and accurate in portraying this—the *Halifax Morning Chronicle* reported, "It is true that in certain circles the project [confederation] is popular, but the idea of Confederation after all is little more than sentiment." The profound statement would ring true in a few short days at Charlottetown; without this sentiment, it is quite probable that the Canadian overtures in Charlottetown might have fallen on deaf ears of unsentimental Maritimers.

Nova Scotia's governor MacDonnell made a revealing comment on the Canadians' six-day visit to his province: "The visit must be regarded as having had, and as being intended to have had an influence on the deliberations at Charlottetown...that Her Majesty's Government must expect to find Confederation of the British North American provinces more extensively supported than was at all probable six months ago."

Fine sentiment also prevailed in New Brunswick, where the press wrote fondly of the Canadian contingent's recent visit to that province. One paper wrote: "The Canadians are good fellows and a jolly set and we are sorry to part with them."

Part they did—in both Nova Scotia and New Brunswick—but only for a brief interlude. Time enough for the Maritimers to reflect upon friends from Canada now familiar to them. The die was cast. The conference in Charlottetown, just two weeks hence, would be something of a reunion, no longer entirely with strangers but with political comrades. The Maritimers may not have known it, but the seeds of budding nationalism—call it sentiment if you will—had taken root.

CHAPTER 5

North and South: The Tallahassee *Affair*

Soon after the Canadian ensemble departed Halifax for Canada, their Nova Scotian hosts got back to the business at hand. The party had afforded all those involved with a short escape from reality; perhaps this partly explained the love affair that developed among the participants. Wartime conditions often give rise to such immediate and intense relationships, and in British North America there was a war going on—political warfare.

For three years by now, Americans had been engaged in a bloody Civil War, which pitted American against American—the Union forces in the North versus the Confederate forces in the South. By the summer of 1864, Unionist forces appeared to have the upper hand and the Confederacy was reeling. The Southerners were desperate for any military success which might raise flagging spirits and bolster the Confederate cause. Ever so briefly, they would find that flicker of hope beyond the American border in Halifax.

Britain and thus her colonies assumed a position of neutrality during the American Civil War; however, this in reality proved to be an illusion. Britain was not prepared to invest in the substantial costs associated with defending her British North American colonies from a belligerent neighbour to the south. On a given day her sympathies may have been divided between North and South. Early in the war the Trent Affair tested British resolve to remain neutral and very nearly brought that nation into confrontation with the Union. It was the first of a series of diplomatic incidents that caused sabre-rattling in Britain and United States.

On November 8, 1861, two Confederate diplomats—James Murray Mason and John Slidell—were making their way to Britain and France to lobby for diplomatic recognition of the Confederacy and to seek financial as well as military support for the Southern cause. The American blockade of all southern ports made for a perilous passage, in this case for passengers on-board British Royal Mail packet RMS *Trent*. Captain Charles Wilkes of the USS *San Jacinto* learned of the Confederates' presence aboard the British vessel and intercepted it with

USS San Jacinto *and* RMS Trent

shots fired across the bow in the Bahama Channel. The two diplomats were removed from the British ship, which brought immediate reaction in Britain for what it deemed to be a violation of neutral rights and an affront to national pride. Tensions ran high, and ultimately President Lincoln, not wishing to risk war with Britain over the matter, released the two envoys without any formal apology.

Two years later, in December of 1863, the *Chesapeake* Affair once again brought Britain and the United States to the brink of hostilities. On the seventh of that month, Confederate sympathizers in Nova Scotia and New Brunswick in a daring act captured the American steamer *Chesapeake* while voyaging off the coast of Cape Cod. They needed coal, and facing odds at Saint John, charted a course for Halifax, avoiding detection by American warships along the way. *Chesapeake* was brought into Sambro Harbour, where efforts were made to provision her with coal. (Ironically, it was exactly fifty years earlier, in 1813, that Halifax Harbour had been the scene of another drama involving an American ship bearing the same name. During the War of 1812, the Royal Navy frigate *Shannon* triumphantly returned from Boston with her American prize USS *Chesapeake* in tow.)

During this time two American warships, USS *Dacotah* and *Ella and Annie* appeared on the scene, the latter arresting two Nova Scotians and one New Brunswicker who remained on-board the *Chesapeake*. This action, in British waters within sight of Halifax, was a violation of British sovereignty and international laws. Britain was offended. Nova Scotians were outraged. At a pivotal moment in the contest of wills, it was said of Premier Charles Tupper that he was prepared to have the guns from Citadel Hill fire upon USS *Dacotah* if she made any attempt to make off with any Nova Scotian prisoners taken from *Chesapeake*. The matter was eventually smoothed over, but only after prominent Halifax businessmen, notably William Johnston Almon and Alexander Keith, demonstrated their true Confederate colours by aiding and abetting the pirates' escape.

Nova Scotia's sympathies were predominantly with the underdog South during the conflict. Bluenoses profited from the conflict, taking advantage of the Confederates' decimation of the North's merchant navy, with increased shipbuilding and greatly expanding profits from the sale of fish, lumber, and coal attributable to high prices generated by a wartime economy. (Halifax's history is said to always prosper in times of war and languish in peacetime.) Southern blockade runners, smugglers, adventurers, and agents flooded Halifax during the hostilities. There was money to be made, and wily Halifax merchants were quick to exploit the opportunities, befriending the southerners in the process.

All the while, the British colonies watched the progression of the Civil War to the south with a wary eye and a certain unease. It was no secret that the loose-knit colonies were virtually defenceless in the face of an emerging giant across the border. According to the *Halifax Chronicle* of September 22, 1864, there they perceived "the fall of the great Republic," fearing repercussions of which might expose the fragile colonies to assimilation or annexation by a United States that could emerge from the Civil War "chafed, angry, and entertaining feelings of mortal hatred and revenge."

It was against this backdrop on August 18, 1864, that the Confederate commerce raider *Tallahassee* steamed into Halifax Harbour with Union gunboats in hot pursuit.

The *Tallahassee*, formerly a blockade runner named *Atlanta*, was purchased by the Confederate States and converted into a cruiser or commerce raider to destroy Union shipping. She was new—and fast. Built in London, England, (which did not endear Britain to the Union cause) ostensibly for the Chinese opium trade, she was commissioned

CSS Tallahassee

in the Confederate States Navy and readied for sea under the command of John Taylor Wood. He was a prominent figure in his own right—the grandson of President Zachary Taylor and a nephew of Jefferson Davis, then president of the Confederate States of America. He would prove to be the ideal choice for command of the new raider.

Captain Wood, born and raised in the United States, was a graduate of the US Naval Academy at Annapolis, Maryland, where he taught gunnery tactics at the beginning of the Civil War. Despite his Union background, he was sympathetic to the Southern cause and so resigned his commission in the North. In 1861, he received a commission as a first lieutenant in the Confederate States Navy. He would see extensive service under the Confederate flag, during which time he gained a reputation for extraordinary valour and daring.

Wood's new command CSS *Tallahassee* was rakish in appearance with a mast forward and two tall funnels, each accommodating 100 horsepower steam engines, which allowed for a top speed of an impressive 15 knots. It was this superior speed that she often relied upon to outrun enemy ships. Her hull and stacks were painted white and her bottom red. She was 220 feet in length, had a beam of 24 feet, and drew 14 feet and was manned by a crew upwards of one hundred men. She was armed with three guns—a rifled 32 pounder forward, rifled 100 pounder amidships, and one heavy Parrot aft. She was in all respects a formidable raider.

In early August, Commander Wood readied his ship for sea. He placed great confidence in his officers and crew, who were all volunteers from Confederate gunboats on the James River and North Carolina waters. His orders read: "The character and force of your vessel point to the enemy's commerce as the most appropriate field of action, and the existing blockade of our ports constrains the destruction of our prizes."

Captain John Taylor Wood

Commander Wood did not disappoint his naval masters. Under cover of darkness on August 6, 1864, he guided *Tallahassee* out of her home port of Wilmington, North Carolina, and past the Union warships blockading the harbour. From here he made his way north, terrorizing commercial shipping all along the eastern seaboard. The casualties would mount to an impressive thirty-three vessels, of which twenty-six were destroyed and seven others bonded or released after capture.

The *Halifax Morning Chronicle* of August 19, 1864, reported that "between Sandy Hook [New York] and Cape Sable several small craft fell a prey to the vigilance of the cruiser and near the latter place she took and destroyed seven vessels and landed their crews at Yarmouth, Nova Scotia." Three more small American schooners were taken and burned between Cape Sable and Halifax with their crews put ashore at some point along the Nova Scotia coast. This remarkably successful campaign against Union shipping, coming as it did just before the capture of Atlanta by Union forces, provided a temporary boost to flagging morale in the South. It was effectively the last victory the South would sustain.

Tallahassee was a steam vessel, and thus her effective cruising range was limited by the need to take on coal. As she approached Halifax with Union gunboats in pursuit, she was low on coal. Halifax being a neutral port, Commander Wood believed this would be a safe refuge, so he navigated her into Halifax Harbour on the morning of August 18. Her arrival caused considerable excitement among the Halifax townsfolk. Shortly after dropping anchor, she was boarded by several "eager inquirers, all burning to hear fresh particulars of her daring and successful career." Among the first of those to board was Benjamin Weir, a local businessman who was the Confederate agent in Halifax. That afternoon *Tallahassee* was towed by the tug *Neptune* over to Woodside wharf on the Dartmouth shore, and during the evening took on a large quantity of coal from the Prussian brig *Marie Griesswold*, which had arrived a few days earlier from Bermuda.

The captain did not receive the welcome he had anticipated. Instead he was greeted with a certain cold politeness by government and naval officials in Halifax who were intent on maintaining at least a posture of strict neutrality; and so the customary courtesies extended to Confederate officers were dispensed with on this occasion. Commander Wood found himself and his crew in a hostile environment. He was served with notice from the lieutenant-governor to depart within twenty-four hours after taking on no more than a hundred tons of coal, just enough to make the passage back home to Wilmington.

A diplomatic tug of war ensued. The prediction in the *Halifax Citizen* of August 18 that "the arrival of this redoubtable craft here has doubtless set the telegraph ticking in many Northern offices today" would soon ring true. The Americans immediately used the office of M. M. Jackson, the American consul in Halifax, to express outrage over the safe refuge offered the rebel cruiser by British authorities. They were of course smarting from the havoc wreaked upon Union shipping along the Atlantic coast by *Tallahassee*, and rightly suspected she was in Halifax to take on more than coal. So in an early dispatch from the American consul Jackson addressed to Premier Charles Tupper, they made it clear they wanted her detained:

> Sir,
>
> I have the honour to inform you that a vessel called the Tallahassee which has for the last few days unlawfully been committing depredations upon the property and commerce of the people of United States, by burning and destroying vessels and property belonging to the citizens, is now on this port.
>
> As this vessel is now here for the purpose of procuring a supply of coal, and also, as is supposed, of arms and ammunition for the purpose of committing further depredations of a similar character, I have respectfully to request the interpositions of the Provincial authorities to prevent her from procuring either coal or arms and ammunition; and inasmuch as the depredations committed by the Tallahassee have been not only in violation of the law of nations, but of the municipal laws, both of Great Britain and of the United States, I have respectfully further to request that she be detained in this port, under proper guards, until further evidence of the facts here submitted can be adduced.

The unwelcome appearance of *Tallahassee* in Halifax was now fomenting a diplomatic incident and threatening the fragile neutrality between United States and Britain. Ironically, it was not only "property and commerce of the United States" that had fallen victim to the Confederate raider. A number of vessels sunk or taken were owned and manned by Maritimers trading with the United States. If there was any outrage over this by provincial authorities it was well disguised.

There followed a series of rapid exchanges in Halifax between representatives of the Crown and of the United States. Premier Tupper deferred to the lieutenant-governor as representative of the Crown in his terse response to the American consul Jackson:

> *I am directed by His Excellency the Lieutenant Governor to acknowledge the receipt of your letter today and to say in reply that His Excellency does not consider it his duty to detain the Tallahassee, or any man-of-war of a belligerent State, on the chance of evidence being hereafter found of her having violated International Law, and that in the absence of proof to that effect, he cannot withhold her commander the privilege of obtaining as much coal as may be necessary to carry her to a port in the Confederate States without violating that strict neutrality which he is bound to observe.*
>
> *I am charged further to say that if any proof or circumstances of strong suspicion can be shewn that arms or ammunition are to be supplied here to the Tallahassee, His Excellency will take adequate precautions to prevent such supplies being furnished.*

While the official reception was formal and frigid, some prominent Halifax businessmen extended a warm and helpful hand to the ship. Benjamin Wier and Company provided coal for her bunkers. The popular Halifax physician and well-known Confederate sympathizer William Almon supplied a replacement for the broken mast on the ship, which had been carried away from collision with the large ship *Adriatic*, one of its hapless victims. In fact, the need for a mast was likely no more than an effective ruse orchestrated by Captain Wood in an effort to further delay his departure until he and his ship could escape under the cover of darkness.

The Halifax newspapers made much of the event, with townspeople taking in every word and watching to see if the Confederate raider would be confronted by Union warships. Excitement mounted with each passing hour, accentuated by rapturous press. Although there were differing reports as to how captive crews were treated aboard the raider, the preponderance of evidence suggested that Captain Wood was very much the southern gentleman, showing every kindness towards his unhappy guests. The Halifax press demonstrated considerable respect for Captain Wood and his crew. An article in the *Halifax Morning Sun* on August 19 was entitled "A Distinguished Visitor," certainly not the sort of description one would use to describe an enemy.

Captain Wood knew that federal gunboats were gathering at the mouth of Halifax Harbour to bar his escape. Two federal ships, the *Nansemont* and *Huron*, were reported to be lying in wait. While *Tallahassee* had superior speed to her advantage, Wood knew that an engagement would inevitably result upon his departure from the safe confines of Halifax Harbour. Time was running out. Naval authorities in Halifax offered Wood a naval escort out of the harbour to the three-mile territorial limit. He wisely refused, believing it would surely lead to confrontation with the Union gunboats. Instead the captain would make good his escape in a dramatic fashion in the dark of night, which has since become part of Halifax's maritime folklore.

While the raider took on coal at Woodside, Captain Wood used this time wisely. He carefully surveyed Eastern Passage, a narrow and shallow channel separating Lawlor Island from the mainland. If he could navigate his ship undetected through this virtually unchartered waterway, he might just succeed in gaining open water and avoid detection by the Union gunboats waiting off the entrance to Halifax Harbour proper. It was a big gamble. If *Tallahassee* grounded, her fate would be sealed. However, Wood was never known to back away from a challenge; he lived by the maxim risk and reward, and took the gamble. Having secured the services of Jock Fleming, a pilot familiar with the local waters, Captain Wood took advantage of a high tide and with the ship in total darkness, pushed off from the Woodside wharf the night of the nineteenth, carefully inching his way up the crooked channel. It is testimony to the skills of both captain and pilot that *Tallahassee*'s hull never touched bottom before the cruiser reached Devils Island (where she dropped off the pilot Fleming as well as two stowaways) before making speed into the open waters of the Atlantic.

In the days that followed, there was considerable speculation as to the whereabouts of the raider. In fact, Captain Wood used the one hundred tons of coal taken on at Halifax judiciously. He made directly for home. On the night of August 25, *Tallahassee* ran into Wilmington Harbour and anchored under the guns of Confederate Fort Fisher. She was closely pursued by the federal gunboat *Monticello* with several shots exchanged, but *Tallahassee's* speed saved her yet again.

Tallahassee had made good her escape from Halifax with no time to spare. Lieutenant-Governor MacDonnell described the events that followed in an August 23 dispatch to Hon. Edward Cardwell, British Secretary of State: "About noon the following day [20th] the United States gunboat *Pontoosuck* [sic], Commander Stevens entered the [Halifax] harbor and lay off York Redoubt, whilst, as I understand, five other Federal cruisers were met or seen at no great distance outside, being a portion of a fleet of thirteen which had immediately started from the United States ports on receiving by telegraph information of the *Tallahassee's* arrival at Halifax. It would seem therefore that the latter had a very narrow escape."

Soon after the *Tallahassee* Affair, the Civil War ended with the surrender of the Confederates. Wood was briefly taken prisoner, then escaped to Cuba before making his way back to Halifax, where he took up full-time residency. At his adopted home, the "cold politeness" with which he had been greeted as captain of *Tallahassee* was replaced with unabashed admiration and camaraderie. The former Confederate cruiser captain opened up a business on the Halifax waterfront from which he proudly flew the Confederate flag. He became one of the city's prominent citizens, raised his family there, and upon his death in 1904 at the age of seventy-three, the *Morning Chronicle* eulogized him as "a Southern gentleman, who would be long remembered for his daring exploits and contribution to the British Empire." He is buried in Camp Hill Cemetery together with his wife, Lola.

It appears there was a certain romance and intrigue associated with Confederate raiders like *Tallahassee*, which frequently were seen in Halifax, usually to take on coal, during the Civil War. There was a kind of reverence espoused by the press while the raiders were in port, but once they had disappeared over the horizon, they were often painted in a different light. This was true too for *Tallahassee* when, on August 22, readers of the *Halifax Morning Sun* were reminded of the dark side of the raider's mission: "It is worthy of note that of the first victims of this destroyer were vessels

John Taylor Wood's headstone in Halifax.

laden with coal from Cape Breton, bound to the United States, and it will be a great bar to the Americans sending for coal to this Province when such a shark is not only upon our coast, but petted and comforted by its inhabitants. We greatly fear that such one-sided and hostile feeling to the United States will be long remembered to our disadvantage."

This was the very sentiment that prevailed in the Maritime provinces as the premiers prepared to discuss the merits of Maritime Union—the underlying fear of repercussions, perhaps even annexation by the United States in the post–Civil War era. CSS *Tallahassee* had been a fresh reminder of the argument for forming some sort of a united front in the face of a perceived threat of annexation by the United States. During the last days of August 1864, the intense excitement generated first by the appearance and followed by the disappearance of the *Tallahassee* was soon forgotten.

In Nova Scotia, New Brunswick, and Prince Edward Island, premiers and other delegates went about making last-minute preparations for Charlottetown and the anticipated conference ostensibly on Maritime Union. Also fresh in the minds of both Nova Scotia and New Brunswick delegates were the fond memories of new friendships so recently made with their Canadian counterparts during the social visits to Saint John and Halifax. Acquaintances and comraderies were about to be renewed in the Prince Edward Island capital.

CHAPTER 6

Circus Act in Charlottetown

‖‖

Prince Edward Island's first inhabitants, the Mi'kmaq, called it *Epekwitk*. The pronunciation later changed to *Abegweit*, meaning "resting on the waves," an apt description, given the island's location in the Gulf of St. Lawrence. Jacques Cartier discovered the island during his first voyage to North America in 1534. It was called Île Saint-Jean while part of the French colony of Acadia. The British obtained the island from France under the terms of the Treaty of Paris in 1763. For a short while, the island was called St. John's Island, until in 1799 it was renamed Prince Edward Island.

Prince Edward Island is geographically small. Since its separation from administration by Nova Scotia in the late eighteenth century and with the establishment of its own governor, lieutenant-governor, council, and assembly, the colony enjoyed political clout as one of the three Maritime provinces in British North America. It is Canada's smallest province, containing a mere 0.1 per cent of Canada's land mass and a mere 0.4 per cent of its population. In 2016, the island had a population of less than 150,000. Interestingly, there are a number of place names on the eastern half of the island prefixed with the word "mount," which belies the fact that the highest elevation on the island is in the range of five hundred feet.

Its history, at least until recently, has been influenced by two issues that have dominated life and politics on Prince Edward Island. Of the two, the land issue would appear to have been the most rancorous. Shortly after Britain assumed control of the island, Surveyor General Samuel Holland devised a plan for the entire island which, given its small size—150 miles in width and approximately 40 miles in breadth— proved to be a modest challenge. He created sixty-seven townships of twenty thousand acres each. A lottery was held in 1767 with the result that most plots were granted to military officers and others the British government owed favours to. Settlers became tenants of proprietors, most of whom never set foot in the colony. Confrontation between the proprietors' agents and the tenants frequently led to violence, with any attempts to change the system blocked in England. By the mid-nineteenth century, local government had achieved a degree of success in buying out some of the landowners, but the question of land distribution and ownership remained a predominant political concern from 1767 until Confederation.

Religion has also played a significant role in the evolution of life and politics on the Island. The modest population has traditionally been fairly evenly split between Catholics (Irish descent) and Protestants (Scottish descent). Traditionally this divide has been reflected in not only the church but also in schools and the press. In many respects the insular nature of living on an island, which only since 1997 has had a fixed link to the mainland, has resulted in a parochial lifestyle in Prince Edward Island. Its residents are independent-minded, and its politicians have always been quick to protect the Island's way of life and political institutions from any perceived external threats. This stance would weigh heavily in Prince Edward Island's position on the Confederation proposal.

It was towards this cultural climate that delegations of politicians from Nova Scotia, New Brunswick, and Canada set forth to meet in Charlottetown in the waning summer days of August 1864.

The return of the provincial steamer *Queen Victoria* from the Saguenay River to the Queen's Wharf at 6:00 P.M. on August 3, 1864, with Governor General Monck, Lady Monck, and party went largely unnoticed by the Quebec citizenry. After ensuring that his eminent passengers were safely disembarked, Captain Pouliot, his officers, and crew immediately resumed their regular duties of supplying the lights and maintaining navigational aids on the river in service of Trinity House of Quebec, which continued its mandate of policing the river.

As recently as August 25 an advertisement under the heading "Trinity House" spoke to the important oversight and administrative function that organization continued to exercise: "Captain Topping of the steamer *Quebec* and Captain Belledeau of the steamer *John Bull* were on Monday last severally fined the sum of £10, the former for passing over and displacing, the latter for displacing buoys in the River Saint Lawrence."

The *Queen Victoria*'s return to active service of Trinity House was short-lived. Within a few short weeks the tug steamer and Captain Pouliot were once again called upon to provide government transport—on this occasion to transport the delegates from Canada to a conference at Charlottetown. Neither Captain Pouliot nor his group of Canada's foremost politicians could have foreseen how this voyage would forever transform the steamer and her role in Canadian history.

Towards the end of August, *Queen Victoria* was taken out of her regular service and made ready to take on a party of eleven, all men, collectively referred to as the Canadian ministry. The core group of eight, representing both francophones and anglophones included Attorney General John A. Macdonald, from Canada West; Attorney General George E. Cartier from Canada East; Minister of Agriculture D'Arcy McGee; Solicitor General H. L. Langevin, from Canada East; Minister of Finance A. T. Galt; Executive Council President George Brown; Provincial Secretary William MacDougall; and Commissioner of Crown Lands A. Campbell. Accompanying this entourage were three others: Executive Council clerk W. H. Lee; H. Bernard, secretary to the Attorney General; and a stenographer, Mr. Charles Drinkwater.

If there is any truth in the saying that politics makes strange bedfellows, then this unlikely group must be said to have given credence to the adage. As discussed, for the past number of years politics in the Province of Canada had been divisive. The "great experiment" to meld predominantly French interests in Lower Canada with English interests in Upper Canada in a single province had not worked. The result was years of political gridlock and failed coalition governments. By the summer of 1864, politicians from both Canada West and Canada East had found one common cause—and one possible way to resolve their political impasse. They were united in their views that confederation may provide the way out of their political stalemate. Desperate times give rise to desperate measures.

On Monday evening, August 29, the Canadian conference guests embarked at Quebec aboard *Queen Victoria* and set off down the St. Lawrence on their joint mission towards Charlottetown. They went well prepared for their engagement. For weeks, the Canadian invitees had spent time preparing for the role each would play in presenting their collective argument on the advantages of confederation to their unsuspecting Maritime hosts. They were all extremely able individuals and seasoned politicians. With their common bond and singular focus, they represented a force to be reckoned with.

The voyage downriver proved to be a most pleasant experience. It afforded the Canadian contingent time to hone their presentations in anticipation of the pending conference and to relax aboard the steamer, where great effort had been made to provide for every comfort of the guests. It was in many ways an adventure. Most in the contingent had never been to the maritime colony of Prince Edward Island, nor its capital. While somewhat uneasy about just what they might expect of their hosts upon arrival, they were nonetheless very confident in their own abilities to "make their case" if given the opportunity. Having already succeeded in inviting themselves to the conference, and, armed with carefully drafted briefs on the merits of the notion of confederation, it simply remained to rekindle that same camaraderie between Canadians and Maritimers that had been so prevalent in the excursion to the Maritime provinces just a few weeks earlier.

One thing was evident from the recent enjoinder of both Canadians and Maritimers: their common appetite for good food, drink, and entertainment. With all these elements present, anything was possible. The Canadian guests carefully planned their strategy to act as hosts to their Maritime hosts when the occasion permitted, using *Queen Victoria* as their floating hotel. To that end, a great volume of foodstuffs and champagne—$13,000 worth of bubbly, worth more than $100,000 in today's currency—was taken aboard *Queen Victoria* before leaving Quebec. It was a staggering amount when one considers that total expenses incurred by the steamer for the Prince of Wale's excursion on the St. Lawrence in 1860 cost a mere $2,500! It was quite a different cargo manifest than the lighthouse equipment, supplies, and buoys normally carried by *Queen Victoria* while in the employ of Trinity House of Quebec. The provincial tug steamer *Queen Victoria* had now taken on the character more like a Canadian "Confederate Cruiser," as the Charlottetown press would coin her. She and her passengers were coming to Charlottetown well-armed.

For the next two days, *Queen Victoria* followed her now familiar passage down the St. Lawrence, favouring the south shore and its bold scenery, past the legendary place names of Rivière-du-Loup, Trois-Pistoles, L'Islet au Massacre, Le Bic, all resplendent in the late August sunshine. Details of the voyage are scant. One brief account is found in a letter from the newspaperman George Brown, who when writing to his wife, Anne, said of the journey:

> We had great fun coming down the Saint Lawrence—having fine weather, a broad awning to recline under, excellent stores of all kinds, an unexceptional cook [Brown was obviously accustomed to a higher culinary standard], lots of books, chessboards, backgammon and so forth. Our first stopping place was Gaspe, a

pretty little fishing town in Canada where the population turned out en masse to receive us amid firing of guns and other rejoicings. Mr. Le Boutillier, M.P.P gave us a most hospitable reception at his mansion and conducted us over the great fishing establishments of the place. In the afternoon we sailed out of the beautiful little harbor in the same distinguished manner of our entry. From Gaspe our course was direct to Charlottetown, the little capital of little Prince Edward Island.

Gaspé was much more than a "pretty little fishing town." It was no accident that brought the shrewd Jerseymen to this area. Largely through their efforts, Gaspé became an important centre for the fishing industry; it soon was exporting its products far and wide to many countries including Italy, Portugal, Spain, the United States, and Britain. While in the words of D'Arcy McGee, "the region was hard, iron bound and cold," in the fishing industry at that time it was important enough that eleven countries, including Italy, established consulates in Gaspé.

It had been just four years earlier that the *Queen Victoria* had anchored in Gaspé Bay, having brought members of the Canadian ministry from Quebec City to meet HRH Prince of Wales on the occasion of his visit to Canada. Upon the prince's arrival, the British escort vessels and the HMS *Hero* with the prince aboard, together with *Queen Victoria*, received a royal salute from a battery of guns in front of Fort Ramsay, the home of prominent local merchant and MPP John Le Boutillier. Obviously he was a man of considerable influence, both during the time of the Prince of Wales's visit and now while playing host to the future Fathers of Confederation.

Originally from Jersey in the Channel Islands, John Le Boutillier arrived in the Gaspé Peninsula around 1815, worked initially with the fish-trading firm of Charles Robin and Company, before leaving Robin to open his own business under the name of John Le Boutillier and Company. In time his establishments were to be found all along the Gaspésian coast, and by 1861 he owned 12 ships, 169 fishing boats, and employed more than 2,500 workers. He was a proponent of confederation, lived to see it happen, and died in 1872, after which his business was taken over by his former employer, Charles Robin and Company. In 1975, his house at Gaspé, Le Boutillier Manor, was designated a National Historic Site.

D'Arcy McGee recorded some of his observations of that part of the passage as the steamer coasted around the "Lands End of Canada"—

The Honourable John Le Boutillier

the peninsula which the Mi'kmaq called *Gaspey*. Rank after rank of steep sea cliffs in ancient formations of dark shale and limestone, showing their upturned edges to the sea and dipping inland, created an illusion that somehow the world had tipped to the north. The ship soon veered south to give wide berth to the reefs at Cap des Rosiers, now marked by the lighthouse, one of the Imperial Lights erected by the late François Baby with his tug steamers *Queen Victoria* and *Napoleon III* almost a decade previously. Beyond Percé and Bonaventure Island was the Gulf of St. Lawrence, where the vast dark waters of the whale, seal, and dolphin—"Jacques Cartier's undiscovered sea," awaited.

As the *Queen Victoria* with the political elite from the Province of Canada steamed steadily towards Charlottetown and her date with destiny, delegates from the Maritime provinces were making their way to Prince Edward Island. The Nova Scotian delegates included MPPs Provincial Secretary Charles Tupper; Attorney General William A. Henry; Adams G. Archibald; and MLCs Jonathan McCully and Robert B. Dickey. They travelled by stage from Halifax to Pictou, where on the afternoon of August 31 they embarked the steamer *Heather Belle* to cross the Northumberland Strait.

The New Brunswick representatives, also a group of five men, included MPPs Provincial Secretary Samuel L. Tilley; Attorney General Johnston; and John H. Gray; and MLCs William H. Steeves and Edward B. Chandler. Later on that same day, they were picked up and taken to the Island by the steamer *Prince of Wales*.

Unbeknownst to all the delegates, Canadians and Maritimers alike, their reception and accommodation in Charlottetown would be influenced by the big top. The Slaymaker & Nichols' Olympic Circus from the United States had arrived and set up tents on an abandoned lot at the south corner of Queen and Fitzroy Streets, just a stone's throw from the Colonial Building on Richmond, the chosen venue for the pending conference. The circus opened on August 30 and was booked for four days. The timing could not have been less opportune.

Charlottetown was then, and remains to this day, a very small place as cities go. It was incorporated as a city in 1855, then a community of 6,500 people. By 1864, its population had increased modestly to about 7,000—a town small in number but large enough to excite and attract an internationally acclaimed circus. The interest in this event was even more widespread. For weeks the local press had advertised special excursions on Prince Edward Island steamers for those who could be enticed to come to the Island from Nova Scotia and New Brunswick to take in the show. Come they did, by the boatload. Charlottetown was ready to party. It had not entertained a circus for twenty years and the last big event was the Prince of Wales's visit in 1860. Residents and countless visitors filled the streets of Charlottetown as the delegates unwittingly steamed their way towards their conference destination.

There is little written about the planning that went into the conference at Charlottetown. This is perhaps a good thing. Secrecy dominated the political meetings so it isn't surprising that little was said or done to make arrangements for the Canadian and Maritime visitors upon their arrival in the host city. Charlottetown only had about twenty modest-sized hotels and inns to accommodate visitors. By August 31, pretty much all the available accommodation had been filled by those who had come to take in the circus. The delegates—the political elite of British North America—would soon find themselves left to their own devices for living arrangements when they stepped ashore in Charlottetown. For some, billeting with their Island hosts would keep them off the streets.

The Prince Edward Island host delegation, as with Nova Scotia and New Brunswick, comprised

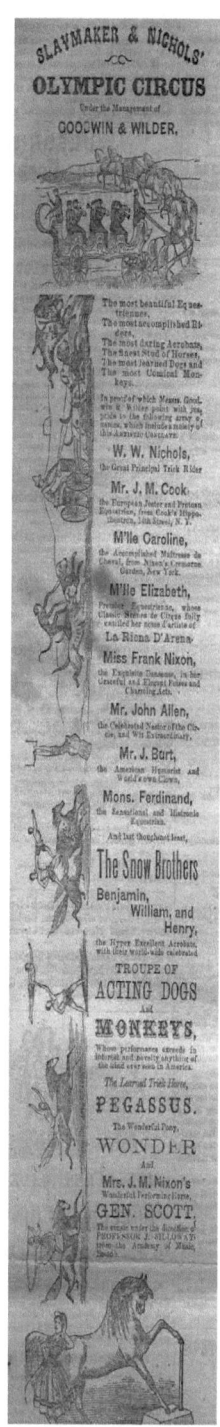

A newspaper advertisement for the Slaymaker Circus.

five men representing both government and opposition in the local assembly. The Island delegation was anchored by MPPs Colonel John Gray (soon to be president of the convention), Provincial Secretary W. H. Pope, and George Coles; MCL Attorney General Edward Palmer; and the youngest of all delegates, Andrew A. MacDonald.

Prince Edward Island was a reluctant and disinterested host of the conference that ensued. As mentioned, Maritime Union, while often talked about in the three Maritime provinces enjoyed little public support and lacked any enthusiasm, even among the most ardent advocates. The movement never really took hold. Prince Edward Island was the least enthusiastic of all the provinces; it saw the movement quite realistically as the annihilation of its cherished independence. Although Islanders were prepared to give it "courteous consideration" (and thus adopted a resolution to consider it along with similar resolutions passed in the assemblies of Nova Scotia and New Brunswick), their overriding desire to maintain their local government always precluded favouring such a union.

During the course of debate in the assembly over the resolution to discuss Maritime Union, the Leader of the Government Colonel J. H. Gray expressed indifference to his own resolution, a reflection of Island obstinacy on the subject: "If the Provinces of Nova Scotia and New Brunswick were to be annexed to Prince Edward Island, great benefits would result to our people, but if this Colony were to be annexed to those provinces the opposite might be the effect." And, in a transparent attempt to inject an element of humour into his argument, Gray stated:

> Is Charlottetown or Summerside to be the capital of Cabotia or Acadia or whatever the country may be called. Are we to be the Ottawa of the united Provinces, and are buildings to be erected here costing as in Canada millions of dollars? Then again, when are the sessions of parliament to be held? Are we to be required to keep our representatives at some Capital in one of the sister provinces from autumn to spring or are they expected to clasp pole in hand and leap from iceberg to iceberg across the Northumberland Strait in the dead of winter. All these questions would be required to be answered before I would be prepared to say whether it would be expedient or not to enter into the proposed Union.

Prince Edward Island's intransigence would ultimately sound the death knell for any hopes of Maritime Union. The reception accorded to the delegates upon arrival in Charlottetown was in many ways a reflection of the Islanders' lack of interest in the question of Maritime Union.

The first delegate from the mainland provinces to arrive at Charlottetown on August 31 was R. B. Dickey, the Reform leader in the Nova Scotia Legislative Council. He was followed by the remainder of the Nova Scotian delegates who arrived aboard the *Heather Belle* from Brule later in the afternoon. According to the *Examiner* newspaper: "Not a soul belonging to the Government was on the wharf to receive them—there was not a carriage of any kind—not even a truck to take their luggage to the hotels or boarding house; and they were suffered to find out by rule of thumb where they could get something to eat and a bed to lie upon. Evidently they managed to make their way to the Pavilion."

The paper was equally critical of the reception given the New Brunswick delegates who arrived around 11:00 P.M. the same night aboard the *Prince of Wales* from Shediac, when "neglect and indifference was measured out to them…with beautiful impartiality." Maybe. The paper didn't say as much, but the inference is that many of the Prince Edward Island government officials who might otherwise have been on hand to welcome the visitors were in fact attending the circus.

It appears to have fallen to Provincial Secretary W. H. Pope to escort the New Brunswickers to lodging in the Mansion House. Saint John's *Telegraph*, the only off-Island newspaper to attend at Charlottetown, in

A sculpture of PEI Provincial Secretary W. H. Pope on the Charlottetown waterfront.

an effort to make light of the situation, reported on the obvious truth—that Charlottetown was full of visitors who had poured in to see not the conference but the circus. This inundation of visitors to Charlottetown was not because "the whole Island population clamorous for a Union were flocking to Charlottetown to enforce their views on the minds of the delegates, but because the inhabitants were travelling, many of them a distance of 60 miles to see the circus."

It was an auspicious start to the proceedings, and one which became even more bizarre the next day with the arrival the Canadians. On Thursday, September 1, the *Queen Victoria* delivered the Canadians safely to Prince Edward Island. Once again, George Brown can be thanked for providing an account of that morning. An early riser, up at 4:00 A.M. to watch the sunrise and to take a saltwater bath, he observed: "We had just reached the Westerly point of Prince Edward and were running along the coast of as pretty a country as you ever put your eye upon. The land all along the shore rises gradually up from the sea for a space of two or three miles and this slope all around the island is well cultivated and when we passed was clothed in bright green verdure. About noon we came to an inlet of the sea amid most beautiful scenery, we came suddenly upon the capital city of the Island."

CHAPTER 7

Assault on Charlottetown

Charlottetown was named the capital of St. John's Island, as it was known, by King George III, after Charlotte, his wife and consort. The colony was renamed Prince Edward Island in 1799 in honour of Prince Edward, Duke of Kent and father of future queen Victoria when he was Commander-in-Chief for North America.

Charlottetown as a colonial outpost played an important role in the struggle between Britain and France for dominance in North America. While under French rule in 1720, fortifications were built on the southwestern side of the harbour and named Port-la-Joye. After the British seized control, the fort was rebuilt in 1758 and renamed Fort Amherst in honour of General Jeffrey Amherst. In 1770, Fort Amherst was abandoned as a fortification and moved to Charlottetown.

In spite of the fort's presence, the city then as in 1864 seemed defenceless to attack from the sea. The last assault on the capital had been in 1775, during the American Revolution, when privateers from Massachusetts attacked the city, taking hostages and, symbolically, the colonial seal. It was a bloodless attack with both hostages and seal later released in Boston.

Ironically, near noon on the morning of September 1, 1864, many Charlottetowners feared for a time that their city might yet again be under assault from the sea by the Americans. It was admittedly a different time and place, but a period during which there was a perceived threat from south of the border.

As both visitors and residents alike walked the Charlottetown waterfront in the warm morning light, they were confronted with an unfamiliar ship dropping anchor in their harbour. It sported twin black funnels and a black hull. It had only been days since the *Tallahassee* had escaped from Halifax in a dash for freedom—but to where? On this day, there was considerable apprehension in the Island capital that this might in fact be the Confederate raider, and if so, what could be the purpose of her presence here?

Captain Pouliot, being unfamiliar with Charlottetown Harbour and with no prior arrangements made for berthing, quite wisely chose to anchor *Queen Victoria* off the sea wall. The initial unease of the spectators ashore then gave way to incredulity as they watched what appeared to be an emissary from shore approach the mystery ship in an open rowboat. The host Island government was at this moment busying itself with arrangements for the conference that was to begin that day. Rather than have an entourage dockside to greet their Canadian visitors, they delegated one of their own, Provincial Secretary William Pope, to be a welcoming committee of one.

Of course those aboard the *Queen Victoria* were ignorant of this and watched bemusedly from the ship as Pope, dressed in a black suit (standard attire for all conference delegates) and black top hat, was rowed out to meet the Canadians "in an unprepossessing little oyster boat, with a barrel of flour in the bow, two jars of molasses in the stern and with a lusty fisherman as his only companion." As if to add spit and polish to the occasion, the *Queen Victoria* hoisted her flag—her battle colours—the campaign for Confederation had begun.

The local *Ross's Weekly* later made light of this spectacle in describing the welcoming: "He [Pope] made a respectful official visit alongside the Canadian steamer *Queen Victoria* seated on an unclean barrel, and in full command of the imbibing oyster boat propelled by a paddle and an oar. The Stewart [steward or purser] of the steamer, taking the Secretary for a 'Bumboater' said, 'I say skipper, what's the price of shellfish?' But William the Secretary opened not his shell."

No record was made of the words exchanged between Pope and the Canadians gathered along the rail of the steamer to receive the "official oyster boat tender." Presumably, they were made to feel welcome and invited to come ashore after which Pope made a hasty retreat.

George Brown was one of those Canadians taking in the scene from aboard the ship. If he was amused or not he didn't say. He did, however, describe the Canadians' landing in a subsequent letter to his wife: "Our steamer dropped anchor magnificently in the stream and its man-of-war cut evidently inspired the natives with huge respect for their big brothers from Canada. I flatter myself we did that well. Having dressed ourselves in correct style, our two boats were lowered man-of-war fashion, and being each duly manned with four oarsmen and a boatswain, dressed in blue uniform, hats, belts etc., in regular style we pulled away for shore and landed like Mr. Christopher Columbus but who had the precedence of us in taking possession of portions of the American continent."

Once ashore, the insufficient accommodation in Charlottetown for the Canadians was quickly apparent. One can only imagine the conversation between the hapless Pope and the newly arrived "big brothers" from Canada. It all worked out just the same.

George Brown became a guest of Pope in his fine home on Mount Edward Road overlooking the bay. There he was made comfortable in true Maritime tradition and became quite taken by Pope's "large family of strong, vigorous, intelligent and good looking children." Four Canadian guests managed to rent the remaining rooms in the Franklin House on Queen Street, a lodging said to have been "furnished in very superior style" and enjoyed "the patronage of the best class of travellers." John A. Macdonald and the remainder of his colleagues made the *Queen Victoria* their floating hotel for the duration of the conference.

Noted Canadian historian Donald Creighton said this of the debacle that met the Canadians: "It was an awkward beginning. Was it an unhappy symbol of the Canadian's real position? Physically their delegation was half in town and half out in the harbor; morally they were a part, yet not a real part of the conference. Was the whole enterprise to end in embarrassment, irritation and defeat? The first hour or so after the landing at Charlottetown must have been full of painful uncertainties."

The engagement that would become popularly known as the Charlottetown Conference, took place during the week of September 1–8, 1864. The proceedings were "informal but formal"—they were not open to the public, and astonishingly, no minutes or records of any kind were kept. What little that could be gleaned from the events of that week would later be revealed from the letters of George Brown, the accounts of Charles Tupper, and the often second-hand accounts that appeared in the press.

The Fathers of Confederation gathered outside Province House in Charlottetown, 1864.

Province House, Charlottetown, in 1864.

From the very outset, what was planned to be a meeting of Maritime premiers to discuss the potential for Maritime Union became a stage on which the Canadian unofficial guests would launch their campaign in support of the larger union for confederation. The conference, which began at 2:00 P.M. on September 1, only retained its mandate for discussion of Maritime Union for as long as it took to select Colonel J. H. Gray, the premier of Prince Edward Island, as chairman and Messrs. Tupper and Tilley as joint secretaries. Then, incredibly, with word received that the Canadians were now making their way to the Colonial Building, it was hastily agreed that the project of Maritime Union would be postponed until after the Canadians had been given an opportunity to present their views on the larger union.

The Canadians were being given the gavel and essentially the conduct of the conference on a silver platter. They probably couldn't believe their good fortune. And they would make the best of it. As one Island political historian later remarked: "The alacrity and unanimity of this decision manifested the lack of interest in Maritime Union and almost suggested a general sense of relief that an opportunity had been afforded for the postponement of its discussion."

Day one was over almost before it started. With Maritime Union off the table, at least for now, the remainder of that afternoon was spent exchanging greetings and renewing acquaintances among all delegates. Brown wrote, "We were formally invited to be present and were presented in great style to the conference. Having gone through the shake elbows and how d'ye do and fine weather, the conference adjourned to the next morning at 10 A.M. to meet for serious dispatch of business."

The Maritime delegates were perhaps taken unawares, but for the next four days they would become cannon fodder to the broadside levelled at them by the Canadians in their pursuit of the confederation project. Political warfare was on, and Maritime Union would be the biggest casualty.

If the Canadians proved their mettle as effective orators, then Prince Edward Island as the host colony excelled in what Maritimers have become famous for—hospitality. Entertainment, liberally lavished with gourmet food and drink, seemed to be ever-present whenever politicians got together, and this was particularly true of the confederation debate. Each day of the conference, beginning with the first evening, was punctuated with grand soirees and receptions. No expense was spared nor half measures taken to ensure enjoyment by all.

The inaugural social affair was a dinner on the first evening hosted by Lieutenant-Governor George Dundas and Lady Dundas at Government House, a beautiful Georgian-style structure built in 1834 on an original hundred-acre parcel known as Fanning Bank. (Much of the original grant was given to the city of Charlottetown in 1876 for public space and named Victoria Park in honour of the reigning monarch, Queen Victoria.) It was a portent of more lively social events, including both ladies and gentlemen, which would ensue as the week progressed.

The next day, Friday, September 2, began in earnest. Having been granted official standing, the floor was open to the Canadians. At ten o'clock Canada opened her batteries with first George-Étienne Cartier followed John A. Macdonald leading the charge. They were both powerful guns in the Canadian arsenal, speaking, as per their game plan in support of the general arguments for confederation. Cartier was a man on a mission to ensure that the dominant French culture in Lower Canada would be retained as a separate political and cultural identity within a larger union. He proved to be a very effective and persuasive speaker, despite lacking full command of the English language.

After the first blunt barrage from Cartier, John A. Macdonald took to the field. The canny Scot was gifted in the art of reading an audience. This day would be no exception. On this occasion he was not under any influence other than his own passion for the subject at hand. He eloquently massaged the minds of his rapt listeners with a plea for a wider union than their own, one that could move them from being "an assembly of mere petty politicians" to a much higher plane of national statesmen.

There is some confusion in the reporting as to the order of the Canadian speakers, but there is no confusion about the fact that they spoke in a concerted voice on all the elements of a confederation. The speeches tended to be long, some of them, like George Brown's, occupying all of the conference time, which ran from 10:00 A.M. to 3:00 P.M. each day without break.

Comparing the Canadian confederate campaign to a military assault was not by chance. Brown used words to suggest as much in his letters, and both the Charlottetown and Saint John press were quick to make this analogy. The *Telegraph* commented on the effects of the Canadian oratory upon the Maritimers:

> New Brunswick, Nova Scotia and Prince Edward Island have all been within the range of her [Canada's] big guns since Friday morning last, and great it is said has been the effect. Indeed her ordnance is of a superior kind, and embraces such well known pieces of artillery as the Cartier, the Brown, the MacDonald [sic] and the Galt....I am told that the speeches have been able and powerful and the arguments almost irresistible. Furthermore... our own delegates are still more favourable to (BNA) Union than they were, and as they consult and converse with the Canadians, the difficulties in the matter of detail vanish.

It can be presumed that the Maritime delegates were by then favourably disposed towards the larger union concept, even before the Canadians completed their presentations. That would become all the more apparent the next day, Saturday the third, after listening to Alexander Galt explain how the new nation's finances would work and the colony's debts would be settled, and promptly at three o'clock retiring to the *Queen Victoria* for a late lunch. While the atmosphere was most casual and convivial, this function was orchestrated by the Canadians, who were only too happy to pick up the tab. The Canadians were firm believers in the maxim that "splendid intoxication was splendor sufficient for ordinary mortals, newly acquainted, and engaged in portentous public business." By the time "lunch" ended late that evening, the Canadians' conquest for confederation was virtually a sure thing.

It was Friday afternoon, the work of the week, albeit a short one, was over. Everyone was in a party frame of mind. The *Queen Victoria* provided the perfect venue, away from the prying eyes and ears of townsfolk, and being hosted by their Canadian guests, the PEI delegates were afforded a brief few hours' respite from entertaining. The commodious hold of the steamer, normally full of navigational buoys and lighthouse materials, was opened. Cases of champagne were extracted and as the afternoon wore on, the bubbly and the conversation flowed freely.

George Brown, ecstatic over the reception aboard *Queen Victoria*, wrote:

> *When the conference adjourned, we all proceeded on board our steamer and the members were entertained at luncheon in a princely style. Cartier and I made eloquent speeches—of course—and whether as a result of our eloquence or of the goodness of our champagne, the ice became completely broken, the tongues of the delegates wagged merrily, and the banns of matrimony between all the provinces of BNA having been formally proclaimed and all manner of persons duly warned there and then to speak or to forever after hold their tongues—no man appeared to forbid the banns and the union was thereupon formally completed and proclaimed!*

There would be a few more days spent around the conference table, with more speeches followed by much more entertainment. However, the midpoint in the convention luncheon aboard *Queen Victoria* is generally acknowledged as "the beginning of confederation." In the view of at least one eminent political historian, P. B. Waite, "Perhaps the greatest single achievement of the conference was the messianic fervor that the converts to confederation were endowed with, and the luncheon aboard *Queen Victoria* visibly marked a stage in that conversion."

It was not the last such function that *Queen Victoria* would host while at anchor in Charlottetown. Each evening provided a different opportunity for the most prominent among the Island delegation to play host to the meeting participants. The conference had by now become so entirely hijacked by the Canadian guests that they were now really more deserving of delegate status.

On Friday, September 2, it was Colonial Secretary Pope's turn to host and he was up to the task. His home was the scene of a *"grand dejeuner a la fourchette"* replete with the Island delicacies of lobsters and oysters. Perhaps he chose to use French to describe the feast in order to appeal to his new friends from Lower Canada.

The memorable luncheon hosted the following day, Saturday, aboard *Queen Victoria* lasted well into that afternoon and was followed later that evening by a dinner hosted by Premier Gray at his home just outside Charlottetown.

Sunday being a day of rest the delegates were left on their own. For the Canadians, it afforded a little down time to regroup and refine plans for completing their presentations.

By Monday the fifth the Slaymaker and Nichols' Olympic Circus had come and gone, and so, too, many of those who had travelled from afar to take in the performances, totally unaware of the historic gathering that had been playing out in their midst. Meanwhile, the caustic newspaperman Brown spent the full day lecturing the delegates on the constitutional aspects of confederation. This topic was no doubt dry enough, so it was both appropriate and fortuitous that at four o'clock everyone adjourned for late lunch at the residence of Mr. Coles, leader of the Opposition. Coles had a life outside of politics—he was a brewer and distiller. Eureka! Thirsts were quenched, backs were slapped, and camaraderie prevailed. Brown, who tended to have a weak stomach and wasn't much of a drinker, later that evening retired to the *Queen Victoria* where he "played chess and caught lobsters over the side of the steamer."

Tuesday the Canadians rested their case and left the proceedings to await word from the Maritime delegates on what course they wished to take regarding Maritime Union. That answer would have to wait until the next morning. In the meantime, the delegates were entertained later that day at the home of Attorney General Palmer, who Brown described as "a very agreeable amicable man—a person of good sense and ability who has seen much of the world." That evening Mrs. Dundas, the lieutenant-governor's wife, hosted a grand ball back at Government House.

Wednesday was the last opportunity for the Maritime delegates to address the issue of Maritime Union. Many of the delegates were prepared to entertain the subject but, in the end, the host colony of Prince Edward Island was "without exception hostile." Generous hosts perhaps, but unflinching and recalcitrant when it came to the subject of union of the colonies. That discussion, such as it was, was now over. The Canadians were invited back into the council chamber and informed by the Maritimers that "they were unanimous in regarding Federation of all provinces to be highly desirable, if the terms of union could be made satisfactory—and that they were prepared to waive their own more limited question until the details of our scheme could be more considered and matured."

The Canadians had done it. While the conference would adjourn for now and pick up in Halifax on September 10, the mission had been all but accomplished. Anything from here forward would be details, aided, as was the expectation, with more of the grape and gourmet.

The *Queen Victoria* had yet to fulfill one more important function. While the Maritime delegates met among themselves that morning, the Canadians waited, but they had already planned to put some of this time to good use. They too were masters of the game of social etiquette. That afternoon they had invited the wives of Dundas, Gray, Pope, Palmer, and Coles, as well as other Charlottetown hosts to be taken by rowboat to the steamer for lunch. It was a nice way of saying thank you to their multiple hosts, specifically the spouses of the gentlemen hosts—and *Queen Victoria* once again provided the ultimate venue for this event. It may not have been quite the spirited affair as the shipboard gathering of the previous Saturday, but it did much to enamour the Canadian ministry in the eyes of the Island hostesses.

Thursday was planned to provide time for all to enjoy the attractions around the Island—"excursion day"—and Brackley Beach proved to be a favourite. Time for salt air and sunshine before the grand finale, a ball given that evening at Province House. Apparently, it was a ball the likes of which the Island had never experienced, before or since. Perhaps it was a release of pent-up emotions arising out of an intense week of political gamesmanship. What better way to end the affair than with food, drink, and companionship born out of political expediency and a circus air.

The Canadians celebrated their victory in promoting the cause of confederation. As for the Maritimers, a kind of euphoria had come over them as the conference progressed, an awakening of a national spirit that took them beyond the constraints of a smaller union and the debate around it that seemed to have no end. Ultimately, the Maritime

An oil painting of the Gala Ball held at Charlottetown's Province House in 1864.

provinces' complacency all but spelled the end of the movement to unify their region. The local press fell silent on the matter—there was no public appetite for union that seemed to be over almost before it started. As Jonathan McCully of Nova Scotia remarked, "It was not merely unfinished, but 'unbegun.' In the early summer of 1864 the Maritimes was in a 'twilight zone' of sorts. There had been no arrangements made for a conference, no venue chosen nor date put forth…in short… nothing." They had been essentially passive participants during a week in which they became persuaded by arguments for a greater cause than their own. They had been sent by their respective assemblies to address the subject of Maritime Union. They were returning home as converts to the cause of confederation, and would now have to account to their own electorate for their actions—or inaction—at Charlottetown.

The closing ball gave a brief respite from that reality, and clearly they didn't want the party to end. The lavish event went on until 3:00 A.M. and took on a character "perilously akin to the worst excesses of the roman Empire." The Charlottetown newspapers took differing views of the occasion. *Ross's Weekly* was the most critical, calling it "a reeking slough of debauchery." There is no doubt that the Canadians long remembered Charlottetown and their Island hosts for their exemplary hospitality. Here they had experienced true *joie de vivre*.

There was little time left for sleep. Near 5:00 A.M. on September 9 the groggy Canadians, Islanders, Nova Scotians, and New Brunswickers— those who had been accommodated ashore—made their way down to the *Queen Victoria* which had steam up and made ready to transport them to Halifax where the conference would continue.

They needn't have rushed. The normally fog-free Northumberland Strait on this morning was "tik-a-fog" and Captain Pouliot wisely chose not to leave the confines of Charlottetown Harbour until 8:00 A.M. He quietly observed his passengers as the anchor was taken up. They were without exception in fine spirits, as they had appeared to him throughout the week. Their mission obviously had been an overwhelming success. He knew instinctively that the ship, his ship, *Queen Victoria* had played a role as a floating campaign headquarters to some momentous event—not yet fully known, but felt all the same. This was apparent from all that had transpired aboard and from the animated conversation of his Canadian passengers gathered under the awning on the fantail of the Confederate Cruiser, as the Charlottetown waterfront receded in its wake. Behind it lay the besieged Island capital and the ruins of Maritime Union.

CHAPTER 8

Mopping Up: Quebec Conference

Before adjourning from Charlottetown, the delegates had agreed to continue the conference in Nova Scotia and New Brunswick. It would appear that both these Maritime provinces wanted the opportunity to try to match Prince Edward Island in extending hospitality towards their Canadian friends.

It was late in the afternoon of September 9 that *Queen Victoria* arrived off the mouth of Pictou Harbour in Nova Scotia. She had been considerably delayed due to the dense fog conditions, which had persisted during the crossing of the Northumberland Strait. She had onboard the entire group, twenty-eight delegates, including a few personal secretaries. Many of the delegates, including the Canadians, were well-briefed on Nova Scotia's rich mineral resources, notably coal and gold. Many had planned to visit the coal mines of Pictou County en route to Halifax. The late arrival by steamer altered those plans somewhat. A party comprising approximately twenty was taken off *Queen Victoria* and transferred to the steam tug *Dragon*, upon which they immediately proceeded to the loading ground at Abercrombie and from there by rail (the first steel rails laid in British North America) to the Albion Mines in Stellarton. They were greeted by the agent Colonel Scott and Mrs. Scott. They evidently were prepared to entertain at their manor at Mount Rundle "in a manner to which his guests had become accustomed."

A correspondent to a local newspaper described the scene:

> The whole party with several additions sat down to a handsome lunch which was awaiting them. Seldom perhaps has the proverbial hospitality of the present Agent of the [General Mining] Association here been shared at one time by so large a number of politically great and distinguished of British North America as graced his board on this occasion, all intent in acknowledging the claims of nature's first law—that of self-sustention, which having been duly cared for, the requisite toasts followed...with Mr. Scott proposing a toast to Colonel Gray, The President of the

convention who, in reply raised his glass in turn to the health of their hostess which it is needless to say was drunk with enthusiasm and handsomely acknowledged by Mr Scott. Soon after Hyde's coaches appeared on the scene and the party packed away for their evening drive to Truro and, with a parting cheer, they drove away from the mansion where they had been so agreeably entertained.

The party left Truro the next morning aboard a special train for Halifax. Along the way they stopped to visit a gold-mining operation "worked by Mr. Buchner who received the distinguished party in the most attentive manner and explained fully the operations connected with quartz mining and gave them a number of handsome specimens."

From there it was on to Halifax and Richmond station. The delegates were met by several members of the Nova Scotia government and deputy provincial secretary. Waiting cabs took them directly to the Halifax Hotel where a luncheon had been prepared.

Meanwhile, other delegates, including John A. Macdonald, Langevin, and McGee had chosen to remain on *Queen Victoria* and enjoy a leisurely voyage to Halifax via the Gut of Canso—long before the building of the Canso Causeway. The *Queen Victoria* with her passengers was tied up in Halifax by the time the overland contingent arrived on September 10. *Queen Victoria* would now have a temporary reprieve from her transport duties while the delegates visited in Nova Scotia and New Brunswick.

The days that followed in both Maritime provinces were for the most part devoted to touring and entertainment. For the Maritime delegates, it was the first opportunity to speak publicly about confederation since their capitulation on the proposal in Charlottetown. Almost without exception they spoke in glowing terms about the future prospects of the larger union. The avowed feelings of good will and euphoria that had pervaded among the participants in Charlottetown continued unabated back home.

The proceedings in Charlottetown had all taken place in camera—the press was excluded. So back home the media could only speculate about what was going on behind closed doors in the Island's capital; editorials both for and against federal union continued. It almost seemed that everyone, press included, had forgotten the fact that their delegation had been sent to Prince Edward Island by resolution of the Nova Scotia

Assembly to discuss the merits of Maritime not federal union. Little wonder if the public was confused about just what was going on.

During this time, the press in Canada were critical at one point of the Maritime provinces "as manifesting a somewhat unfriendly feeling towards Canada." To that suggestion the *Halifax Morning Sun* of September 2 replied: "We [Maritime press] have the right to deal warily in transactions where such weighty and important measures are involved, and we must not be considered unfriendly to Canada because we are cautious in entering into engagements where we may come out second best. *Pro tanto quid retritusonus* [sic] is not a bad motto and we only require an equal share of the good while we assume a proportionate share of the responsibility of the contemplated confederation."

This rhetoric was ramped up even further when on September 19 the same newspaper reported that "a portion of the French Press of Canada is strongly opposed to a Union of the Lower Provinces with Canada. One of the papers, *L'Union Nationale* opposes it in every shape as it fears by such a Union British feeling would have a predominating influence in Lower Canada." To this suggestion the Nova Scotia paper retorted: "The sectional feelings of Canada will in all probability be a bar to anything like a friendly union of that (Canada) province with the lower colonies."

It had to have been a frustrating time for the press. They were anxious for their representatives to return home. In an earlier editorial on September 12 the *Halifax Morning Sun* was still writing under the subtitle "Intercolonial Union" when it reported:

> *The steamer Victoria, placed by the Canadian Government at the disposal of the convention arrived here Saturday with a portion of the delegation, the greater part of them having chosen the overland route, visiting on their way several of our principal mines....*
> *Of course, we cannot speculate upon what if anything was achieved at the sitting in PEI or what the prospects are of a realization of the grand project as the doors were closed, even against the press, but as soon as we are made acquainted with the results of the proceedings we will lay it before our readers.*

The reconvening of the conference in Halifax was marked by a colonial dinner on Monday, September 12, at the Halifax Hotel. The waistcoats of all the delegates must have been getting tight by this time. The dinner was described as "one which might have tempted the appetite of the most abstemious anchorite."

In the soft glow after a fine repast, the speeches followed. In keeping with the mindset that prevailed upon adjournment in Charlottetown, everyone appeared to be *ad idem*, and almost without exception spoke glowingly about the prospects for confederation. It set the tone for the remainder of the Maritime tour, and for the next conference, which had now been determined would be held in Quebec on October 10.

Nova Scotia's lieutenant-governor, much to the delight of the Canadians present, led off by reportedly saying, "He hoped the discussion of the Union of the Provinces would be attended with good results; and he was sure the home Government would throw no object in the way of any project which the united wisdom of the provinces would think conducive to their welfare and prosperity."

Cartier, never one to miss an opportunity to speak, addressed the gathering on the subject of confederation, "which would make them a great and powerful nation; the only thing required was unity in purpose, and sinking all sectional and political differences in order to accomplish this great end."

George Brown followed up with remarks that made light of the recent Canadian conquest in Charlottetown when he opined: "They [Canadians] came here not seeking a remedy for Canadian grievance, but as they [Canadians] were about to reorganize their constitution, they came to invite the Maritime Provinces to join them in a federation, provided that the latter thought that they would be benefited thereby."

True to form, the only contrary view was expressed in few words by Prince Edward Island premier Colonel Gray. In responding on behalf of the Island to the federation proposal, he expressed little enthusiasm for the project, saying that he "had gone as far as his duty warranted."

At least one Halifax newspaper agreed with him. In commenting upon the recent visit to Halifax of the delegates, the *Morning Sun* wrote: "The grand project however now under discussion—a federal union of the provinces—has not we believe been rendered much more probable by this visit, for in the private discussions to which it has given rise, we think we can detect a strong feeling of dislike to such a close union as the Canadians seem so anxious for....We warn our public men not to fall into the error of supposing that at present the people (Halifax is not Nova Scotia) of this Province view the scheme with anything like sufficient favour to consent to it readily."

It would appear that the elected representatives were intent on listening to themselves talk rather than attending to the views of their electorate on this subject. The Canadians may have taken comfort in winning the initial battle, but the war of words over confederation would rage on for another three years.

From Halifax, the Charlottetown Conference—now a travelling roadshow—moved on to Saint John on September 14. In New Brunswick as in Nova Scotia, there were newspapers either opposed to or supportive of confederation. The delegates had no sooner arrived in Saint John when Fredericton's newspaper, the *Head Quarters*, made its take on the import of the Charlottetown meeting known to its readers: "Rumour or report has it that the New Brunswick delegates…were much struck, and they say converted by the arguments of the Canadian ministers. From all accounts it looks as if these gentlemen had it all their own way…and that, what with their arguments and what with their blandishments (they gave a champagne lunch on board the *Victoria* where Mr. McGee's wit sparkled brightly as the wine), they carried the Lower Provinces delegates a little off their feet."

And so they did, and continued to do all the way to Quebec. The few days spent in New Brunswick in both Saint John and Fredericton were little more than opportunities to travel, dine of course, and in the glow of candlelight and wine, pontificate on the seemingly irrepressible virtues of confederation. The spirit of détente born in Charlottetown persisted as the party wended its way through Nova Scotia and New Brunswick. The Canadians remained entirely confident. They had succeeded in capturing the minds of the Maritime delegates in Charlottetown; now it remained to finish the mission in Quebec.

The Canadians left nothing to chance. Their strategy for Quebec was simple. The date of October 10 had already been agreed upon, soon enough to ensure that no momentum would be lost in the campaign. It was important to keep the group focused and together as much as possible. The *Queen Victoria* had been the fulcrum for the group in Charlottetown—why not press her back into service as the floating hotel for the Quebec Conference?

John A. Macdonald took up this initiative, and wrote on September 20, 1864, the following letter to Nova Scotia premier Charles Tupper describing the considerable amenities of the *Queen Victoria* and inviting him and his colleagues to use the steamer as transport to Quebec City.

My Dear Sir;

I am advised by the members of the Cabinet to mention to you that the steam yacht Queen Victoria will be prepared to leave Pictou on Wednesday the 5th of October for Charlottetown—that she will leave Charlottetown on the following day for Shediac—and will leave Shediac on Friday the 7th of October with a view to her arrival in Quebec on Sunday the 9th of October, upon which day the members of the Cabinet hope to have the pleasure of seeing you here.

The accommodation which she will afford is as follows: in the saloon are 8 Staterooms each containing 2 berths, and there are also in the saloon two sofas which, if necessary may be made available for sleeping accommodation.

There is also a large Stateroom under the companion ladder with one berth and one sofa and this Stateroom opens into the Ladies Saloon.

In the aft, or Ladies Saloon are two staterooms each with one berth and a sofa, also two open berths and two sofas.

Upon the deck is a large Stateroom (used in our late trip as a Bath Room) containing two berths….

The following is a summary:
Berths: 23
Sofas: 6
———

 29
a supply of beds and bedding will be placed on board in the event of further provision being necessary for the party.

I am to request that you will communicate to those who may contemplate accompanying you the arrangements made as to the departure of the vessel. I write also to Colonel Gray, Mr. Tilley and Mr. Hoyles to the same effect.
The members of the Cabinet trust that you will find the accommodation to your comfort and they are satisfied that Captain Pouliot will do all in his power to make your voyage enjoyable.

I have the honour to be
John A. Macdonald

The Canadians, employing the quill of the future first prime minister of Canada, had made an offer the Maritimers could not refuse. With fond memories of the considerable comfort afforded by this vessel still fresh in mind, Tupper and the Maritime delegates were quick to accept. Once again, the *Queen Victoria*, dubbed by some Islanders as the "Canadian Confederate Cruiser," was taken up for service by the Canadian ministry as a steam yacht.

So it was that *Queen Victoria* tied up in Pictou on October 4, where she took on the Nova Scotia delegates, as well in some cases their wives and daughters whose presence in Quebec the opportunistic Canadians would press to their advantage. Also accompanying them on this occasion was Nova Scotia lieutenant-governor Sir Richard Graves McDonnell, who it was said "took a deep interest in the union negotiations." From Pictou, *Queen Victoria* once again crossed the Northumberland Strait back to Charlottetown to collect the Prince Edward Island contingent led by Premier Gray and also including some wives and daughters. Much like a dressed-out water taxi, *Queen Victoria* then proceeded back across the strait to Shediac where the New Brunswick delegates, with yet more wives and daughters, boarded the steamer for the voyage upriver to Quebec.

Not all the Island and New Brunswick attendees chose to travel aboard *Queen Victoria*. For whatever reason, the Island's opposition leader and former premier George Coles chose an alternate mode of travel. He, his wife, and daughter took a train from Shediac to Saint John where they met up with New Brunswick premier Sir Samuel Leonard Tilley and other delegates from that province. Together they travelled on the steamer *New Brunswick* down the Bay of Fundy to Portland, Maine, where they took the Grand Trunk Railway northward to Quebec. It seemed an odd choice for travel given the comforts and comparatively seamless transport offered by the steam yacht.

For the larger group aboard *Queen Victoria*, the two-day passage allowed time and opportunity for the Maritime politicians, by now quite familiar to each other, to mingle in the same excursion atmosphere enjoyed just a few weeks before by the Canadian ministry in their trip downriver to Charlottetown. Edward Whelan, the owner and editor of Charlottetown's *Examiner* newspaper was also an Island delegate and witness to the festive mood that prevailed aboard *Queen Victoria* as she progressed along the waterway. He wrote later that until driven inside by gales and snow squalls, the deck of *Queen Victoria* "was seldom deserted by promenaders during daylight and long after dark."

Quebec City was the capital of Canada in 1864. At that time it had a population of about sixty thousand. It was, and remains, a very imposing place, situated on a high promontory overlooking the St. Lawrence River. The *Queen Victoria* arrived in her familiar homeport late on October 9—she had been delayed somewhat by inclement weather, conditions which would continue during the early days of the conference.

All the delegates were put up in the Saint Louis Hotel. The event planners had persuaded the proprietor to remain open beyond the end of the season in order to accommodate the Maritime guests. The Canadian hosts took pains to ensure that there would not be any repeat of the scramble for rooms they had witnessed in Charlottetown. The hotel proved to be very pleasing to the guests who, soon after arrival, "constituted a very merry party." The Canadian budget for the Quebec Conference was liberal. The hotel expenses finally tallied at around $15,000 during the sixteen-day conference. To put this cost into some perspective, *Queen Victoria* had arrived in Charlottetown with a shipload of champagne at an estimated value of $13,000! Just how much of this cargo remained for consumption at Quebec is not known.

However, from all accounts there was plenty of merry-making—augmented by champagne—during these days spent in Quebec and Canada West. By now, the modus operandi of the Canadians was a familiar one, and the press was quick to criticize: "The Canadians who must after all be generous hearted fellows, appear to have great faith in the power of good feed, champagne and torch light, as much more potent than dry argument. They seem to think that turning the head is a synonymous phrase with convincing the mind."

Back in Nova Scotia the media also looked skeptically upon the work ethic of its delegates to Quebec. The *Halifax Citizen* wrote a satirical essay that observed:

> The Intercolonial Union Convention at Quebec gets on with its business swimmingly, having already accomplished a reception at Government House, and a Ministerial dinner or two, besides

several private efforts of the same kind. The members are now in training for a grand Ball to be given in the parliament buildings which will require the most united and patriotic efforts of all the delegates to get through to the satisfaction and honour of the provinces they respectively represent. To give full scope for the display of the powers of the Colonial representatives on this occasion the House of Assembly room is to be cleared for dancing, the library to be furnished for a reception room while the supper is to be spread in the legislative council chamber. After they have accomplished all that is expected of them in the way of balls and dinners and sight-seeing in Quebec, they are to visit Montreal, Ottawa and Toronto and other cities where a round of duties of somewhat similar nature awaits them. It is to be earnestly hoped that they will get through all this public duty without injury to their own health, or to the provinces in whose interests they profess to be employed.

It was hard not to be cynical. However, the Quebec Conference played a most important role in the move towards confederation. By the time the conference convened in Quebec on October 10, 1864, everyone—Maritimers, Canadians, and Quebecers alike—were imbued with a sense of importance: they were acting out roles that just might change the face of British North America.

A historical record of Quebec City many years later reveals of the importance that early capital attributed to the Quebec Conference:

The 10th of October 1864 will be a memorable date in the annals of Quebec. In the historic halls of our Parliament House on mountain hill, there sat for 16 days, with closed doors, the Conference of the Canadian government, with the delegates of the Maritime provinces, under the sanction of the Queen and at the special invitation of her Vice-Roy and representative on our soil, Lord Monck, the Governor General.

It was composed of thirty-three members and was presided over by the premier of Canada, Sir Etienne P. Taché, one of the Aide-de-Camp to Her Majesty. Never before or since has the city witnessed such an imposing Grand Council. All British America had her eyes on the august assembly from whose calm and thoughtful deliberations, a new nationality, combining the hoary wisdom of Magna Charta, with the enlarged freedom of every dweller on American soil.

Closely indeed was this famous national Conference watched by the Canadian—the American—the English Press, but the members having found that their private debates, if published, might lead to misunderstandings and complications wisely decided to proceed with closed doors; this left them much more freedom.

There have been volumes written about the proceedings and import of the Quebec Conference. Its greatest achievement was the serious work given to the details and the resulting seventy-two resolutions hammered out during that time. By the time it wound up on October 16, many of the delegates had spent the better part of three months together. A few months ago they had hardly known each other. Now, after the "maritime ceilidh" of early August followed by back-to-back conferences in Charlottetown and Quebec, they had become best of friends in a common spirit of co-operation and élan.

The Maritime delegates returned home via the most direct route, which was the Grand Trunk Railway from Montreal to Portland, Maine.

The two voyages of Queen Victoria as Ship of State in 1864. (Solid line = first route, August 29–September 19; dotted line = second route, October 2–October 9.)

A map of the Dominion of Canada, 1867.

The extension of rails east from Rivière-du-Loup, long a sensitive issue between Canada and the lower provinces, was finally about to begin.

Queen Victoria by now had resumed her old duties back on the river. Her eminent passengers, including most recently the political elite of British North America—those "pioneers of our nation"—soon forgot *Queen Victoria*. It was fall. The air was brisk, and the trees in full colour. The navigation season on the St. Lawrence was coming to a close but before then, on November 3, records indicate *Queen Victoria* left Quebec that day "for Pictou and intermediate ports with mails, passengers and freight in place of the steamer *Lady Head*." For the remainder of the season she was engaged in towing vessels. On November 28 she went to her winter quarters at Sorel or Louise Basin in Quebec.

While *Queen Victoria* had been employed as a federal cruiser, her sister ship *Napoleon III* had assumed her duties as tug steamer on the St. Lawrence. The latter would go on to enjoy a long career as a working tug steamer on the St. Lawrence, river and gulf, and be remembered as one of the vessels that formed the nucleus of what would become the Canadian Coast Guard Service. The *Queen Victoria*, part of that same nucleus, was destined to take her place in the making of this nation. True to her character she would meet a different fate, one brought about by changing economic times on the mighty river, which she was built to serve.

For the next two years, *Queen Victoria* continued to work the St. Lawrence. During this time the confederation debate continued unabated in the legislative assemblies in both Canada and the Maritime provinces. After Quebec, the Canadians moved swiftly to bring the Quebec Resolutions before the British Parliament for ratification. Britain was anxious to help expedite the concept of a broad federation of the provinces.

There were differing views among Maritimers and mixed appetite for confederation among the home electorate. In Nova Scotia the "anti-confederate cause" was taken up by none other than Joseph Howe. As fisheries commissioner, Howe did not take an active part in the Charlottetown or Quebec Conferences. Instead, while the delegates met to discuss the future of a nation in Prince Edward Island, Howe was in Newfoundland and Labrador performing his government function. Those days he spent travelling to various outports aboard HMS *Lily* must have been difficult for the statesman. One is left to ponder just what difference he might have made, and what the outcome might have been had he participated in the Charlottetown and Quebec Conferences.

The 1865 navigation season on the St. Lawrence began much like any other year. On June 13 *Queen Victoria*, still under command of Captain Paul Pouliot, left Quebec for Pictou, calling at Gaspé with the customary cargo and passengers. However, on this occasion she also carried "a number of men for the Nova Scotia railway." Work on the much sought-after line to Truro was by now under way in an effort to fulfill one of the major campaign promises made by Canadians to the Maritimers. She was no sooner back to Quebec than on June 26 she left for Halifax "carrying a large number of men for the Nova Scotia Railway, being the first regular trip of the Line formed between Quebec and Halifax." A small thing perhaps, but just maybe it appeared she was destined to continue to play a role outside of her tug service in nation building.

It was not to be. Within a year, colonial delegates prepared to take their seventy-two resolutions and case for confederation to Britain before the London Conference. The subsequent royal assent was given to the British North America Act on March 29, 1867. Before Canada became a nation on July 1, 1867, *Queen Victoria*—the Canadian "Confederate Cruiser"—lay at the bottom of the Atlantic Ocean.

Part 3

Attempts to Repatriate Canada's Liberty Bell

CHAPTER 9

The Last Voyage of Queen Victoria

By 1866, Quebec City was feeling the effects of a slowdown in the economy. For the past number of years, it had witnessed a gradual erosion of shipping traffic on the St. Lawrence River to Montreal. By contrast Montreal had continued to prosper after dredging of the river and harbour, which resulted in increased shipping, much of it to Quebec City's detriment.

The economic downturn impacted commercial activity in the port, and with a decrease in shipping came a corresponding reduction in demand for tug services. The Department of Marine and Fisheries, which owned both *Queen Victoria* and *Napoleon III*, now found itself considering alternative uses for it tug steamers. One option was chartering the steamers for commercial use. The department was already experimenting with using some of its tugs as "excursion steamers." In July advertisements appearing in the *Quebec Gazette* notified the public that the steamer *Advance* under command of Captain Simard would depart the provincial steamer's wharf on the twelfth, "offering a delightful and refreshing salt water excursion" to patrons.

The newspaper commented on the attractive look and new type of service now offered by the *Advance*: "We notice with pleasure the fine appearance of this boat. She has been newly painted and fitted up for the comfort of parties seeking a salt water excursion and we are sure that under the new management this vessel as well as the other provincial steamers will become more remunerative and quite popular, as it is allowed by Mr. Huot and the other gentlemen connected with the Provincial steamers office spare no pains to accommodate the public."

Meanwhile on the other provincial steamer, the *Lady Head*, Captain Marmen remained on her customary schedule with regular departures from Atkinson's Wharf in Quebec to the lower ports via Gaspé, Percé, Paspébiac, Dalhousie, Miramichi, Shediac, and Pictou.

There had also been recent attempts from within the private sector to create and expand upon trade opportunities between Quebec and the lower Provinces, as Nova Scotia, New Brunswick, and Prince Edward Island were known. Early in August a "new and handsome steamer," the *Union*, was put into service by the St. Lawrence Tow Boat Company. It was purpose-built for the commercial run between Quebec and the Maritime provinces. Her inaugural trip downriver was a precursor of things to come. It was reported by an interested and vigilant local press that "*Union* had lost $1,700.00 by her first trip to the Lower Ports and that owing to the small quantity of freight offering, government will have to grant a subsidy or the line will be discontinued."

This prophecy came to be true; within a matter of days the company announced that it was withdrawing *Union* from the fledgling service. Interest in advancing trade between Quebec and the lower provinces was not restricted to the Quebec public. In the Maritimes, the media—which had not witnessed such an effort to expand trade between Canada and the lower provinces since failure of the *Royal William* in the early 1830s—went on the attack. The first editorial in the *Halifax Citizen* appeared September 8: "We are informed that the fine new steamer *Union* has been withdrawn from the line between Quebec and Pictou. The reason for this is not yet assigned but it is probably owing to the fact that she is too expensive for the existing trade on the route, and that the Canadian government have refused aid by way of subsidy."

The same paper confirmed this to be the case in a subsequent editorial of September 15, 1866, headlined "Steam in the Gulf":

> By late Canada papers we learn that our surmise as to the cause of the new steamer *Union* being withdrawn from the Quebec and Pictou route was correct: she was withdrawn owing to the government having failed to give the support which is considered necessary for a Line of fast streamers on this route, until such time as a self-sustaining trade can be developed....It is understood that the *Napoleon III* will take the place of the *Union* for the remainder of the season, running alternatively with the *Lady Head;* but this ship does not give the accommodation either to freight or to passengers that the route now requires and it certainly seems to be a short-sighted policy on the part of the three provinces interested to allow such a steamer as the *Union* to be withdrawn from the service.

The *Halifax Morning Chronicle* was even more critical in an extensive editorial on September 25 entitled "Trade Between Canada and the

Maritime Provinces": "The question of steam communication between Canada, New Brunswick and Nova Scotia is just now largely engaging the press of Montreal, Quebec and Toronto. It is admitted on all sides that the effort recently made to establish a regular and permanent line between Quebec and Halifax by the St. Lawrence Tow boat company has resulted in a miserable commercial failure." The paper then cited the *Quebec Daily News*, which had proclaimed that "the failure to establish intercolonial trade and commerce through means of direct communication must be charged to the Canadian government and to it alone....The government not only failed to foster such a trade but has thrown every conceivable obstacle in the way. It seems that for the same postal service for which *Lady Head* received $800.00 (subsidy), the Canadian government had the modesty to offer the owners of the *Union*, which was recently taken off the route, the insignificant amount of $120.00."

Perhaps more could have been done to foster intercolonial trade on the St. Lawrence. It was easy to blame government, then, and to this day. At this time, Confederation was still a year in the future; British North America was still made up of colonies independent from each other. And there was no denying that the Maritime provinces up to this point were still very content with their trade links, which moved product north and south, not east and west. Canada and its capital Quebec chose a different course to foster trade. Following the example of the Maritimes, Quebec determined to open trade relations with the West Indies, and more particularly Cuba.

In 1865–1866, the Confederate Council of Trade in Canada and the actively participating provinces had extensive communications with officials in the West Indies, Brazil, and Mexico about prospects for expanded trade. Cuba was among those countries that had been receiving a lot of attention. There were differing views on the advantages of establishing trade with Cuba, but the Canadian press appeared generally supportive. Towards the end of August, the *Ottawa Citizen*, under a headline "Canadian Trade with Cuba," wrote:

> *A Canadian merchant whose action was suggested and guided by the West India Trade Commission has just returned to Canada after a visit to Havana which occupied 21 days and cost him $260.00. He has brought back orders for 200,000 box shooks, 2 or 3 cargos of hay, 100,000 feet of white pine lumber and an assorted cargo of lard, furniture, black oak, beans and yellow corn. The fine sugars*

> from Havana are always exported in boxes. The boards are cut up into the proper length and a set of pieces for one box done up into a "'shook." The quantity of boxes commissioned in Cuba every year is immense. A single transaction like the above more than repays the country for all the expense of the commission…and the fact that the journey of the merchant in question was a direct result of the commissioner's report is an abundant answer to assertions that it (the report) was full of trash and nothing else.
>
> The Report is one which every merchant ought to have in his office and we are glad that the printing Committee of the House have decided on printing immediately a second edition of 3000 copies.

Then, on August 20, a royal decree issued by the Spanish government ordered that all export duties would be lifted on the island of Cuba. Export and import duties were very much part of the ongoing negotiations with West Indians, and this regarded as a very positive step towards enhanced trade.

These circumstances may have been brought about the curious development that unfolded with *Queen Victoria*. The Canadian government decided to charter her to Quebec businessman T. C. Duplessis. His plan was to take a cargo of "Canadian produce" to Cuba and return home with a cargo of tobacco, cigars, and fruit. There was a big demand for cigars in Canada, and Cuban cigars fetched a good price as "the best of the best."

No one could have foreseen it at the time, but the voyage was doomed to fail, much like the fortunes of the food crop in the St. Lawrence Valley that year. Throughout the summer months of 1866, prospects ran high and there was every expectation for a bumper crop that year. The newspapers reported regularly on the state of the harvest, and during the early part of the summer there was every reason to believe this would be a good year. In July the *Quebec Gazette* reported glowingly on "The Season and the Crops": "We have to report a continuance of weather every way favourable to the labourers and hopes of the farmers. Frequent, yet not too copious rains, accompanied by warm growing temperatures have wrought like magic upon crops of all kinds." And just a few days later, the same paper rejoiced: "The countryside looks beautiful, the warm weather having given a wonderful impetus to vegetation, and altogether we think it may safely be predicted that the gloomy fears about a deficient harvest which prevailed earlier this season will not be realized."

Good weather, good crops, highly touted trade opportunities in Havana, as well as the recent lifting of duties in Cuba, all these factors very likely gave rise to Mr. Duplessis's decision to charter a steamer from the Canadian government. The wheels of this venture, once in motion, were unstoppable. Almost from the time the decision to charter was made, things changed—notably the weather.

As summer progressed the weather deteriorated into some of the worst ever recorded. The newspapers, previously so optimistic, were now despondent in their coverage of the crops. By the end of August, the *Gazette* was reporting that "there appears to be no end to the rainy spell which has prevailed for some days past and unless dry weather speedily sets in, the most gloomy apprehensions are entertained respecting the growing crops. As it is, we fear that a very large portion of this season's hay has been destroyed."

The situation hadn't improved by the waning days of summer. In September the *Gazette* was even more pessimistic with reports that "grain was rotting on the ground and in some places it will not be worth carting into the barn. The straw also has become almost dung. Never before in our memory have we witnessed so long-continued a term of wet weather. For several weeks we have not had a day on which rain did not fall. It seems now to be very generally admitted that a large part of our crops in Lower Canada and even in Central Canada are so damaged as to be past recovery."

It appears that the potato crop along the St. Lawrence was particularly hard hit. This along with cabbage "and other vegetables" represented the largest component of the cargo that Mr. Duplessis had contracted to take to Cuba. Given the foods' condition and perishability, there was mounting concern it might not survive the trip. *Queen Victoria* was designed to transport navigational aids and lighthouse supplies—and sometimes, when the occasion warranted it, champagne—not produce.

Initial plans had the *Napoleon III* taking the charter to Cuba. On the last day of August the *Quebec Gazette* wrote that the post office had served notice of mails for Havana, direct on the *Napoleon III*. That same day an advertisement appeared in the newspaper under the name of the postmaster John Sewell: "A mail for Havana, Cuba, direct, *per Steamship Napoleon III* will be closed at this office on Saturday the 8 of September next at 2:30 P.M." The prepaid postage rates were quoted at twenty cents per half ounce and three cents each on newspapers. Plans changed between then and September 5, when an identical advertisement ran in the *Gazette* substituting *Queen Victoria* for *Napoleon III*. Perhaps it was just an oversight—we'll never know.

While Mr. Duplessis finalized arrangements for his cargo, Captain Pouliot prepared for the voyage ahead. This was a very real departure from the movements of his ship during the past ten years, all of which had taken place in and around the St. Lawrence River and Gulf of St. Lawrence. Now, for the first time since her delivery to Quebec from Scotland, he would take *Queen Victoria* out into the Atlantic—to the West Indies and back—in the fall of the year. If he was apprehensive, he did his best not to show it. Just the same, he would be glad to see this charter through and bring *Queen Victoria* back home for winter layup.

Queen Victoria left Quebec for Cuba on September 10. Her only scheduled stop was at Pictou "to take on passengers if any offer" through the local agent Mr. A. P. Ross. She arrived in Pictou on the thirteenth, after experiencing heavy winds en route. It was to be a portent of things to come. Her cargo was reported to include potatoes, cabbage, and "other assorted vegetables." Interestingly the Pictou shipping extracts for that day reveal that *Napoleon III* was also in port on this date. *Queen Victoria* took on coal and at noon the following day departed for the West Indies. She would never be seen again in Canadian waters.

There is little written about the passage south. She had taken on sufficient coal in Pictou to complete the voyage without stopping and arrived in Havana around September 23. She was there only long enough to discharge her cargo and take on "cigars, tobacco and fruit." As a trade mission the voyage was a commercial failure. The *Montreal Trade Review* would later report: "It was learned from Havana that commercially the enterprise in which the *Queen Victoria* was engaged had resulted in loss. The cargo which consisted of cabbages and potatoes, owing to the bad condition in which these vegetables were put on board had become rotten and unsalable. Had it been in a saved condition a considerable profit would have been made."

If that wasn't bad enough, September was hurricane season in the Caribbean. Captain Pouliot was anxious to leave for home. There were no weather forecasts, or any established means of communication. The transatlantic cable had just been successfully laid between Ireland and Newfoundland, but this was of no advantage to those in the West Indies. It was just plain bad luck that 1866 would go on record as one of the worst years for cyclones. And one of the strongest to ever be recorded was brewing as *Queen Victoria* was made ready for sea.

The first few days out from Havana were uneventful. By October 1 *Queen Victoria* was steaming some 230 nautical miles off the coast of North Carolina and Cape Hatteras, which had a well-established reputation as a "graveyard of the Atlantic." Unbeknownst to Captain Pouliot, to the south the Bahamas was being ravaged by "one of the most dangerous, destructive and enduring hurricanes to ever make its trek across these archipelagic island." Winds at 140 miles an hour had left half of Nassau devastated and 387 people dead. The winds increased as the storm moved north over open waters towards *Queen Victoria*.

Many vessels of all types and sizes would fall victim to this weather event, which would inflict damage all along the eastern coast of the United States and British North America and Newfoundland. Two of the many casualties, the British-registered *Queen Victoria* and the American steamer *Evening Star*, occurred unknowingly within a short distance of the other. The American steamer would receive coverage in the international press for weeks afterwards, while *Queen Victoria* would soon be forgotten, becoming a mere statistic of countless ships lost at sea.

The *Evening Star* was an American paddle steamer of 2,200 tons and length of 275 feet, sailing regularly between New York and New Orleans. On September 29 she left New York with 270 people aboard, including about 100 "courtezans [sic], most of tender age, engaged to spend the winter in New Orleans." The passenger list also included 59 members of the French opera troupe of Paul Alhaisa. They and most of the others aboard would never reach their destination. The purser, Mr. E. S. Allen, who survived, described the days prior to the sinking. After crossing Sandy Hook bar exiting New York, the ship initially encountered strong easterly winds and a heavy swell. This had moderated by the following day and the seas were smoother. October 1 they were off Hatteras with calm weather and a clearing sky. "The 2nd opened with a fresh breeze from the east south east with a high running sea. Towards evening the wind increased to a gale and by midnight a hurricane was blowing and the ship lying helpless in the trough of the sea."

Evening Star was some miles to the south of *Queen Victoria*, about 180 nautical miles east of Tybee Island, Georgia, when she foundered and sank about 6:00 A.M. on October 3. There were only seventeen survivors. The press had a heyday with the story, making much about the seaworthiness of the ship and the inadequacy of her lifeboats.

The USS *Tahoma* was more fortunate. This naval vessel managed to weather the storm and safely reach Nassau, where Lieutenant Commander William Gibson was confronted by the hurricane's devastation upon the island capital. The account of his experience sheds light on the maelstrom that *Queen Victoria* sailed into:

> On the 3rd and 4th inst., when on a line between the Bermudas and Hatteras, we encountered a revolving storm of hurricane violence. We are not in distress but the damages sustained were serious. As carefully computed from the observation the cyclone was moving northeasterly at the rate of 13 mph. Its centre when near to us was lat. 33 N, long. 72.40.20 W, bore SSE 40 miles distant.
>
> It came upon us suddenly and with little premonition, the barometer registering rather than foretelling the changes of wind and weather. The sea rose so rapidly and grew so dangerously heavy and confused that, being satisfied we were in the left hand semi-circle of the storm, I deemed it safe to abide the issue by having the Tahoma brought to on the port tack.

The *Daniel Webster*, another American ship, was abandoned in the storm. Her captain made the following observation, which gave credence to the suggestion that where a vessel happened to be in the circumference of the storm dictated whether or not its crew and passengers survived: "The hurricane was of the cyclone kind and from observations before and since, its diameter was not more than 100 miles—based on the fact that vessels in different positions on the circumference of a circle of that diameter have suffered, whilst others within and without the circumference have escaped."

The *Queen Victoria* was in the wrong place at the wrong time with nowhere to hide.

The most accurate account of *Queen Victoria*'s fate is found in the *Quebec Gazette* of October 15, 1866:

The steamer Queen Victoria was on her return from Havana to Quebec with a cargo of cigars, tobacco and fruit, a crew of 36 men and 6 passengers.

On Thursday the 2nd the weather looked very threatening and preparations were made for a storm which commenced about 9 o'clock that evening and soon increased until it became a hurricane. Such was the searching fury of the wind during the night that, although the sails were all lashed to the spars, it tore away the greater part of them from the fastenings and blew them away in ribbons. In the morning some pieces of the mainsail were seen fluttering about in ribbons and the topmast broken. The vessel at this time was off the coast of North Carolina about 230 miles out at sea.

The storm continued the whole of the night and the following day and about 7 o'clock was at its highest. At this time the foremast broke and the debris were cut away. The sea was then breaking over the unfortunate steamer and Robert Day, the first mate was washed overboard. The storm continued during the day but abated in the afternoon. It was then believed and reported by the sailing master that they were all safe, that the steamer had weathered the storm. But it was soon afterwards discovered that she had sprung one or more leaks and was making water in some place or places unknown. To keep it down the pumps and buckets were resorted to with all possible energy. But these exertions were insufficient and the water continued to gain. The pumps were not in the best of order and to some extent became choked.

The fires [boilers] were threatened the morning of the 4th and there was no longer any hope of saving the steamer. She had two boats [lifeboats], but both, had they remained in good order, would not have been sufficient to hold the 42 persons on board. One of them however was smashed to pieces during the night of the 3rd and the remaining one had a hole stove in it. In this state of things, with death staring all on board in the face, a brig was descried at about 10 A.M. when a signal of distress was hoisted. The brig saw it and immediately lay to.

The remaining boat was now patched up for the temporary service of removing the crew and passengers to the brig, and this, with the aid of the brig's boats as well, was affected in safety although the sea was still high.

The brig proved to be the Ponvert, Captain Allen from St. Mark's Florida, bound for New York, and nothing could exceed the kindness with which the rescued persons were treated. But one unfortunate, the second engineer, Henry Bailey died soon after removal on the brig. He appeared to be a strong man, but working below, near the furnaces, almost naked, with nothing but a pair of trousers on, from the great heat he rushed upstairs several times to see how things were proceeding above, and in his heated, unprotected state the seas breaking over the vessel washed over him again and again. The result was a violent congestion of the lungs and he died.

The Queen Victoria sank at about 3 o'clock on the afternoon of the 4th in 76 degrees 30 minutes west longitude and 33 degrees 3 minutes North latitude. Very little of the clothing even of the passengers and crew was rescued and nothing else. The vessel was not insured at Havana, but it was at Quebec, in different American offices for $33,000.00.

The rescued passengers remained on the brig for two days when all of them except five were taken on board the steamer James A. Geary [sic] for Baltimore.

Captain Stevenson, the sailing master of *Queen Victoria*, plus three of the crew and one passenger remained aboard *Ponvert*, which continued on to New York. From there everyone dispersed never to be heard from again.

On October 9 a report out of Fort Monroe, in Chesapeake, Virginia, noted: "The steamer *James A Geary*, from Wilmington, N.C., bound to Baltimore was spoken to in the Chesapeake Bay yesterday afternoon by the quarantine steamer *City of Albany*, Captain Armsworth. She reported having onboard the Captain, crew and five passengers, 35 in all of the British steamer *Queen Victoria* which foundered at sea October 4th, during the recent hurricane."

Even while *Queen Victoria* was slowly sinking, the hurricane continued its passage north along the eastern seaboard. It cut a path of destruction as it went. The *Morning Chronicle* of November 8 reported that in the month of October seventy-seven vessels of all kinds belonging to, bound to, or from ports in United States were totally lost or missing, among them *Queen Victoria*.

When the news of the sinking eventually made it back home, newspapers in both Canada and the Maritimes expressed regret for the sinking, but only in terms of the lost trade opportunity. On October 10 the *Quebec Gazette* first broke the news:

> *The telegraph today announces the loss of the provincial steamer Queen Victoria which left here the 8th of September last on an experimental trip to Cuba. She had disposed of her cargo of Canada produce and was on her voyage back with a return cargo when she foundered in a heavy storm on the 4th inst.*
>
> *The sad event is to be deplored, not only for the melancholy loss of life, but for the unfortunate check it gives to the opening up of a new channel for our trading enterprise.*

Shortly afterwards, the *Halifax Citizen* commented on the "Loss of Queen Victoria": "It will be remembered that an attempt was made some time ago to establish steam communication between Canada and Cuba. The *Queen Victoria*, the pioneer of the Line, started on her first trip from Quebec about the middle of September calling at Pictou on her way. The attempt to establish a new trade has met with a serious repulse by the loss of this vessel."

The suggestion arose that because she may not have been seaworthy "some further inquiry [should be] made" into the sinking of the *Queen Victoria*. The Quebec press claimed that as a Clyde-built ship, one of Robert Napier's own masterpieces, it "ought to have been in all respects seaworthy. But it is plain that her boats [lifeboats] and appliances [pumps] were insufficient for so severe a test, and it is plainly more owing to the mercy of Providence than the discretion of men that there is a survivor to tell the tale. The brig which rescued the crew and passengers weathered precisely the same storm and did not lose her sails, her masts and her boats."

Part of this observation is true. It was just good fortune that *Ponvert* appeared on the scene when she did. But for that, and without any lifeboats, very likely everyone aboard would have perished. However, it is not necessarily true that *Ponvert* endured the same hurricane conditions, particularly when one considers the comments of other mariners as to the size and circumference of this hurricane. A few miles may have made all the difference between survival and succumbing to the tempest. The *Queen Victoria* was built as a tug steamer for use on the St. Lawrence River and gulf, comparatively quiet inland waterways when contrasted with the tempestuous Atlantic. She was indeed sturdily built. During her ten-year service as a tug, she had towed hundreds of vessels up the St. Lawrence, many of much greater tonnage than her own. The stresses and strains on her frame would have been considerable. She had already undergone a major refit to replace her engine frames, which had weakened as a direct result of hard use. There is every reason to think that the cyclonic conditions she endured off Cape Hatteras might well spring leaks in her otherwise tight hull. Whether the pumps were in good working order is a matter of conjecture. Once the fires in her boilers were doused, and without any sail, the ship was at the mercy of the sea.

As so often happens, tragic events of considerable import are overlooked and quickly forgotten as a result of other important and newsworthy developments or conditions of the time. For instance, the death of the great pioneer of steam on the Atlantic, Halifax's Samuel Cunard, hardly received mention in the press, which at that time was preoccupied with covering the assassination of US president Abraham Lincoln. The sinking of the Canadian Pacific liner *Empress of Ireland* in the St. Lawrence River was obscured by wartime conditions in 1914. The equally tragic and even more significant loss of the Cunard flagship *Lusitania* to a German U-boat in 1915 was relegated to the back pages in favour of other wartime coverage.

Queen Victoria suffered the same fate. Just about the time word of her loss was trickling into the press, on October 14 a disastrous fire crippled Quebec. That story would dominate local press while *Queen Victoria* quickly faded into history.

CHAPTER 10

Rescue and Retribution

Maine, the home of the rescue vessel *Ponvert*, was formerly part of the French colony of Acadia. As such it shares a rich history with the neighbouring Maritime provinces of Canada. Gouldsboro, Maine, the place where *Queen Victoria*'s memory would be immortalized, was incorporated in 1789 and celebrated its 225th anniversary in 2014. It is known today as a beautiful gateway to the Schoodic Peninsula of Acadia National Park:

> The original name of Acadia National Park—Sieur de Monts National Monument—recognizes the ongoing influence of the French explorers who visited the area in the early 1600s. In 1763 the Seven Years' War between France and Great Britain for control of North America ended with a British victory. With peace came bold pioneers seeking opportunity.
>
> The first recorded non-Native American settler on the peninsula was Thomas Frazer who built a salt works at the mouth of a creek that today bears his name. Another early settler was the town's namesake Robert Gould whose untiring efforts and boundless optimism helped attract new members to the growing community. By the early 1800s Gouldsboro was a thriving town of lumber and grain mills, fishing and shipbuilding.

Prospect Harbor is one of a number of fishing villages that comprises the larger town of Gouldsboro, Maine. *Ponvert* was built in Prospect Harbor by master-builder Sherman Smith in 1863. It was one of a number of brigs built in the area during the mid-1800s, which included the *Ruby*, *Chastelain*, and *Sullivan*. A brig is a sailing vessel with two square-rigged masts. They could vary in length from 75 feet to 165 feet, and depending on the size would carry a crew of ten to fifteen seamen. During the Age of Sail, brigs were turned out by the thousands from shipbuilding yards, which were to be found in virtually any modest cove or harbour in the New England States and the Maritime provinces. Considered the workhorse of the lucrative West Indies trade, brigs were commonly

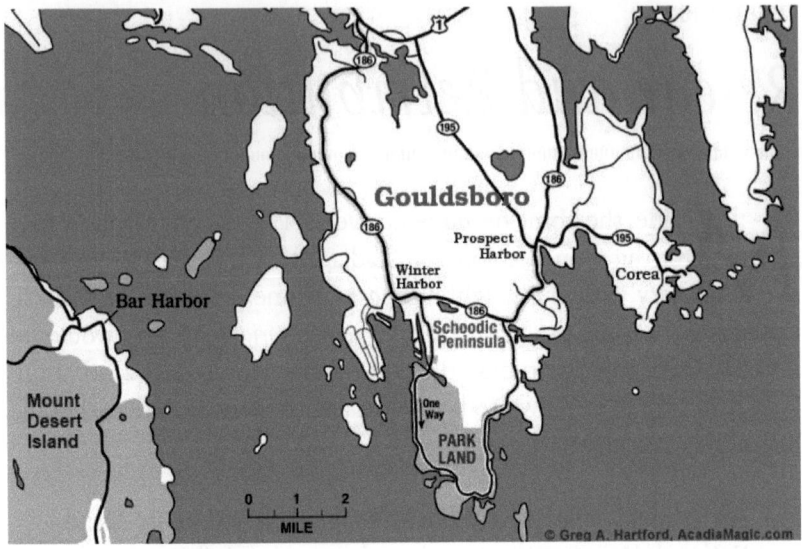

A map of Prospect Harbor, Maine.

employed, particularly during the last half of the nineteenth century, in the coastal trade to carry goods from Maritime ports and return laden with goods from ports in the Caribbean and South America.

The *Ponvert* was built for Captain Rufus Henry Allen (1827–1910), who was born in Prospect Harbor. The Allen family had strong ties to the sea. Rufus had two brothers, Horatio and George, both mariners. He also produced two sons, Fred Holloway Allen and John Moore Allen, both sea captains.

The name of his ship is curious. It appears to have been taken from a family name, that of E. L. Ponvert, who was manager of the Hormiguero Sugar Estate, an old sugar plantation near Cienfuegos on the southwestern coast of Cuba. During the latter half of the nineteenth century, the United States did considerable trade with Cuba, as sugar was one of its primary exports. The E. & L. Ponvert brothers operated out of Boston, and it is likely that Captain Allen and his vessel were routinely employed in the transport of sugar from Cuba to United States.

In October 1866, Captain Allen aboard *Ponvert* was on a voyage from Florida to New York. He and his vessel had managed to avoid the worst of the hurricane when they came upon the hapless *Queen Victoria* on October 4. By this time the seas were still running high, but the worst of the wind had abated. In keeping with the rules of the sea, Captain Allen shortened sail and hove to upon seeing a distress signal from *Queen Victoria*. It was readily apparent that the steamer was sinking, and Captain Allen immediately dispatched his boats to take the passengers from the distressed vessel. In this manner, and with the aid of one of *Queen Victoria*'s boats, everyone managed to be taken off the stricken steamer. The rescue had come none too soon—*Queen Victoria* sank within an hour of taking off the last person to abandon the ship—Captain Paul Pouliot.

Of the forty-two souls aboard *Queen Victoria*, forty had survived the sinking. The first mate, Robert Day, had been washed overboard during the height of the hurricane while cutting away debris from a broken foremast. He had sacrificed his life to save the ship. Soon after being taken aboard *Ponvert*, *Queen Victoria*'s second engineer, Henry Bailey, died from "congestion of the lungs." Captain Pouliot deeply felt these losses; not only had he lost his ship but with it two of his best, long-serving officers and mates.

The rescue and transfer from *Queen Victoria* to *Ponvert* had taken a few hours. Most escaped with little more than the clothes on their backs—and were glad of it. However, as the lifeboats carried away the passengers, Captain Pouliot, realizing that *Ponvert*'s modest resources would be severely taxed with the addition of forty unexpected passengers, thought to remove considerable silverware and cutlery from his doomed ship to augment that aboard *Ponvert*. As well, his gratitude towards Captain Allen was such that he swiftly arranged to remove and successfully transfer *Queen Victoria*'s 100-pound ship's bell—no mean task in itself—which he subsequently presented to Captain Allen as tangible thanks for saving both him and his passengers. Whatever became of *Queen Victoria*'s logbook remains a mystery to this day. Pouliot's decision to remove and gift the bell was of no particular significance, but time and tide would eventually bring both the bell and the ship back into prominence.

The impact of rescue at sea is felt not only by those fortunate enough to be rescued but often by the rescue vessel and its passengers onboard. Their voyage most certainly, and sometimes the lives of the first responders, are often materially changed by the experience. For *Ponvert*, circumstances brought on by the rescue continued to unfold in the days after the sinking.

For the next two days following their rescue, *Queen Victoria*'s survivors were made as comfortable as possible upon the little brig. As there were limited resources aboard, including food and water, Captain Allen chose to make for the nearest port of Hampton Roads. Before then, however, the American steamer *James A. Gary*, commanded by Captain Charles

Captain Rufus Allen's pocket watch.

Wilson, appeared on the scene. She was hailed by *Queen Victoria*'s sailing master Captain George Stevenson and soon thereafter took aboard all but five of *Queen Victoria*'s complement before making for Baltimore. Captain Pouliot chose to accompany the majority of his passengers on the *James A. Gary*, leaving his next in command, Stevenson, aboard *Ponvert* to assist in the management of the brig.

Now with a much more manageable complement of crew and passengers, *Ponvert* came about and headed off shore to continue her voyage. She soon encountered an easterly gale of sufficient force to drive her ashore. Fortunately, she was able to extricate herself, but only after expending $4,000 for assistance in floating her off the bottom. Besides the exorbitant fee, the salvage men stole much of the silverware, leaving Captain Allen with just the ship's bell and a silver tea service from *Queen Victoria*.

It must have been difficult, particularly for the five passengers taken aboard from *Queen Victoria*, to confront another storm, accentuated by the stranding ashore of the rescue ship. Having survived this calamity, the *Ponvert* did make it to New York, where she discharged her passengers and cargo. What became of those from *Queen Victoria* is not known. Captain Pouliot along with the thirty-four others taken aboard *James A. Gary*, were disembarked from that vessel in Baltimore. From there they eventually made their way back to Quebec, the crew perhaps redeployed in the remaining tug fleet, while Mr. Duplessis returned to his business, only too happy to give up on any further charters to Cuba.

Most of *Queen Victoria*'s survivors had just made their way back home to Quebec when calamity struck in Quebec City. On October 14, 1866, fire ripped through the city, destroying more than 2,500 homes and leaving a staggering 20,000 people homeless. According to the *Quebec Gazette* of October 15, the fire started early in the morning in a grocery store of a Mr. Trudel, located adjacent to the Jacques-Cartier Market: "Quebec has to deplore one of the greatest calamities that ever befell it. Nearly one half of the suburbs of the city is in ashes. All the conflagrations that have taken place of late years pale before this last terrible scourge."

The time of year of this disaster only compounded the tragedy: "Now the winter is almost upon us; the poor laboring classes who resided in the burnt district, after a dull summer [poor crops] have but little provisions made to face the dreary winter months, but this little has in less than one short twenty-four hours been swept away. They are thrown upon the cold charity of the world and unless the benevolent, the rich, and humane come promptly to their aid, suffering and want and disease from exposure must necessarily be the case in very many instances."

Fortunately for Quebec City residents, the humane and not necessarily the rich did respond. Relief efforts began almost immediately with aid coming from as far away as Halifax.

The *grand incendie de Québec*, as it was known, had left the city reeling and people there could certainly be forgiven if they were too preoccupied with their own survival to take note of the recent fate of the provincial steamer *Queen Victoria*.

The ensuing story of Captain Paul Pouliot took on another, more bizarre twist. From all accounts he was the premiere captain in the provincial tug service, having been master of *Queen Victoria* for most of her ten years in service. He was a capable, charismatic, and charming captain who had not only performed admirably in the tug service but also as a host and ambassador to princes and premiers and to Canada's Fathers of Confederation.

After the loss of *Queen Victoria*, Captain Pouliot, like his ship, faded into obscurity. It does not appear that he was given a new command; perhaps there were no openings available to him. Unlike him, Captain Gourdeau, who had been commander of *Napoleon III* for the past number of years, would remain in command for years to come. It is possible that Pouliot, distraught over the loss of his ship and two of his shipmates, may have chosen to "stay ashore."

The next we hear of him, Pouliot is keeper of the Pointe-des-Monts lighthouse on the remote north shore of the St. Lawrence River at Baie-Trinité. The irony of this place name would not have been lost on Captain Pouliot. It had the same derivation and meaning as Trinity House of Quebec, Holy Trinity, which he had served under while in command of *Queen Victoria*. The river and the gulf had been his workplace. His life and experience had been devoted to maintenance and oversight of navigational aids and supplying lighthouses. Now he found himself, isolated and alone, exiled almost, in one of the earliest lighthouses built

The silver service tea set from the Queen Victoria.

in Canada. It was a marked departure from being captain of the *Queen Victoria* and commander of the Canadian Confederate Cruiser to a posting and lonely vigil as keeper of a light on the rocky, forbidding shore of the St. Lawrence. A more remote location could not have been found. In comparison, the forced exile of Emperor Napoleon I to the remote island of Saint Helena was a paradise.

Pointe-des-Monts lies approximately halfway between Baie-Comeau and Sept-Îles on the north shore of the St. Lawrence River. It is at a point where the river ends and the gulf begins and an ideal location for the second lighthouse to be built on the river. The first at Île-Verte, where the Saguenay River enters the St. Lawrence, had been constructed twenty-one years earlier as one of the first projects of Trinity House of Quebec, which had chosen the site and begun planning for a second light as early as 1826. For many years it had felt the need to prevent ships leaving the river at this point from going ashore on Anticosti Island, which had already claimed many unsuspecting victims. In 1828, John Lambly, harbour master for Quebec, urged a special committee of the House of Assembly of Lower Canada to erect a lighthouse at this location. For him Pointe-des-Monts was an idyllic location: "a station formed by nature for a light house, where a light there would serve as a point of departure on the north shore, allowing ships to avoid Anticosti Island, Manicouagan Shoal and the strong southeast current along the south shore."

He made his case. Construction began in July 1828 using limestone brought from Montreal and cladding of firebrick for the outer wall of the tower. When completed in 1830 it was an imposing structure: a tower standing 90 feet tall, with a 40-foot diameter at the base, tapering to 20 feet at the lantern room, which topped the conical tower. The lighthouse has seven floors with entrance gained from the first floor and the upper decks lit by a tier of six rectangular windows, aligned one above the other on both the northern and southern sides.

However ideal for a lighthouse to be situated, Pointe-des-Monts was a very lonely place, inhabited primarily by Indigenous peoples called Montagnais, who lived along the north shore of the St. Lawrence from Tadoussac (mouth of Saguenay River) to Pointe-des-Monts. Prior to Pouliot's posting there, the lighthouse had become not only a beacon for ships but also for the Montagnais. They soon learned that where there were white men, there was rum.

There were only a handful of keepers of this light while it was manned between 1830 and 1983. The first was James Wallace who served for fourteen years. The second keeper and Captain Pouliot's predecessor was Zoël Bedard. He lived in the lighthouse with his wife for twenty-three years and died there in late 1866 or 1867.

Living conditions were far from ideal. The stone tower initially served as the living quarters for the keeper, his assistant, and their families. The ground floor was taken up by a kitchen with a fireplace and oven contained within the thick stone walls. The next five floors served as living area and bedrooms while the seventh housed light-keeping materials. It was neither comfortable nor healthy. Water leaks and dampness were commonplace. On occasion water leaking down through the lantern necessitated moving beds and furniture from the upper levels of the tower.

Perhaps these conditions brought on or hastened keeper Bedard's death. Evidently winter conditions had set in and the ground was frozen when he passed away. His body was kept during the winter months at the station until it could be taken up to Quebec for burial when spring arrived and shipping resumed in the river. It is likely that the new keeper, Paul Pouliot, had assumed his role and had Bedard's frozen corpse as company during his first few months on the job. That would have done nothing to help his state of mind.

Pouliot in fact had competition for the position of lightkeeper. Upon her husband's death, Mrs. Bedard applied to Marine and Fisheries to replace

The lighthouse at Pointe-des-Monts.

her late husband as keeper. In another strange twist, the irony of which would become more evident during Pouliot's management, Mrs. Bedard was informed that she could not be hired "because of her advanced age and because the position of light-keeper must needs be filled by a man whose services are at all times more competent." Pouliot received the posting, although soon his competency would come into question.

It wasn't long after Captain Pouliot arrived on the scene that things started to unravel at Point-des-Monts. The normally friendly Montagnais considered the lighthouse to be haunted and visited by the devil himself, and they stayed away while Pouliot was keeper. He was partly responsible for perpetuating this myth with his own assertions that he had seen a man walking around the turret at night. There were very few other people about and the walls of the lighthouse were very close.

The isolation would have challenged the strongest will, let alone one who was already suffering from delusions and possibly early dementia. There was very little to do other than tend the light. The supply vessel, most likely *Napoleon III*, would only come by once, perhaps twice, a year with supplies. As the sister ship to *Queen Victoria*, her appearance would be a constant reminder to Captain Pouliot of his own loss.

Having so little to do other than tend the light, those unhappy memories would likely have played upon his mind. The most important task, tending the light, was a 24/7 job. During fog and snow the keeper also had to "fire the gun" every hour, day and night. In addition to the lighthouse, Pointe-des-Monts was a provision depot for distressed seamen. As keeper, Pouliot had to maintain and tend to the stocking of those provisions, which in the case of this light would typically consist of a dozen barrels of flour, eight barrels of peas, and seven to eight barrels of pork. During his last year as keeper, Pouliot received an annual salary of $760. This was slightly more than the cost of supplies for that year, which came in at around $600. These included dry goods, chimneys, gunpowder, horseshoes, oats, and repairs.

The Department of Marine and Fisheries Annual Reports for the last few years of Pouliot's tenure provide some early indications that Pouliot was suffering from mental stress. The Quebec agent was first to sound the alarm. In his report for 1871–1872 he noted: "The tower and buildings are in excellent order, not having required repairs for some time. Owing to the present keeper's continued state of ill health a change will soon be necessary."

The change was soon made. In his Annual Report for 1872 the Minister for Marine and Fisheries wrote: "Mr. Paul Pouliot, the keeper of the light at Point des Monts became incapacitated by mental infirmity during last summer for discharge of his duty and was removed from the station and placed on the superannuated list with an allowance of $138.24."

His replacement was approved by an Order-in-Council dated October 26, 1872: "On the recommendation of the Honourable the Minister of Marine & Fisheries, the Committee advise that Mr. Ferdinand Fafard of Bagot Ville, Chicoutimi…be appointed keeper of the light house at Point des Monts at a salary fixed by Order in Council of February 11, 1870 of $700.00 per annum, including allowances, in place of Mr. Paul Pouliot who has become incapacitated by mental infirmity for the discharge of the duties of Light Keeper, and is superannuated."

Pouliot's service was over. In reality, however, life for Captain Pouliot had ended during the tail end of a great hurricane when, on October 4, 1866, he watched as his beloved *Queen Victoria* slipped beneath the waves of the Atlantic.

Of his final days after being removed from the lighthouse little is known. He may have been placed in the marine and immigrant hospital, an institution for "Sick & Distressed Mariners" operated by Trinity House of Quebec. It is also possible that he ended up in the notorious Saint-Vincent-de-Paul Penitentiary in Lévis, on the opposite side of the river from Quebec. At that time both the criminally and medically insane were customarily incarcerated in the same institution for "treatment." And nothing has been found to confirm if he had family. As of 1872 the "Decayed Pilot Fund" (pensions) of Trinity House of Quebec showed an allowance of $80 per annum for a "widow of pilot Paul Pouliot" and a further entry of $16 for a child, J. Pouliot, "infirm." Regardless, it was a cruel and sad end to the career of a fine gentleman and seaman.

The Pouliot name is almost synonymous with the St. Lawrence River. Research suggests that as a family the Pouliots, many of whom came from Île d'Orléans, just downriver from Quebec, constituted generations of master mariners and pilots on the St. Lawrence. In more recent times, and until his retirement in 2010, Captain Michel Pouliot had been president of the Canadian Marine Pilots' Association as well as the International Maritime Pilots' Association. He has been the recipient of many honours, including the Order of Canada. Given his untiring efforts to promote the profession, and through it, maintenance of marine and environmental safety, he would undoubtedly have been a good candidate for master of Trinity House.

Pilotage runs deep in his family. His father was a pilot, as were his two brothers, and now two sons and a nephew. His grandfather, François Xavier Pouliot was captain of the Canadian government steamer *Montmagny*. Much like *Queen Victoria*, she was a lighthouse supply and buoy tender. And, like *Queen Victoria*, she attained fame for services rendered outside her normal operating duties. CGS *Montmagny* was the third of four ships chartered by White Star Line to search for bodies in the aftermath of the sinking of *Titanic*. For a few days in May 1912, she scoured the Atlantic, retrieving four bodies and by the end of that month had resumed her normal duties back in the St. Lawrence River.

The Pouliot family is rich in the maritime history associated with the St. Lawrence, both gulf and river. Captain Paul Pouliot was part of that family and its tradition of unselfish service to a grateful nation.

CHAPTER 11

An Important Gesture

Bells are symbolic—particularly a ship's bell. A ship's bell was normally made of brass with its named engraved on it and often the year of launch. They can be very plain or quite ornate, but regardless of detail, they are always considered a prized possession. In the seventeenth, eighteenth, and nineteenth centuries, the ship's bell was housed in a belfry, often very ornate, forward at the break of the forecastle. In more recent times, it is common to find the ship's bell placed at the foot of the mainmast if the vessel is so configured.

The main use of the bell was to mark the time of day for the crew. As early as the fifteenth century, ships' bells have been used to sound the time on-board ship by striking each half-hour of a watch. The mariner's day is divided into six watches, each four hours long, except that the 4:00 P.M.–8:00 P.M. watch may be dogged, that is to say, divided into first and second dogwatches, each two hours long to allow men on duty to have their evening meal. Through the eighteenth century, time was ordinarily measured on-board ship by using a thirty-minute hourglass. The quartermaster or ship's boy turned the glass when the sands ran through, and it became customary for him to strike the bell as he did so. Eight times in each watch the glass was turned and the number of strokes on the bell indicated the number of half hours elapsed after the men came on deck. These strokes are sounded in pairs with an interval following each pair.

Bells were also struck as safety signals when ships were operating closely together in fog. Ships' bells have ceremonial uses as well. It is a naval tradition to baptize children using the ship's bell as a baptismal font and to engrave the names of the children on the bell afterwards. And so, a ship's bell is a prized possession when the ship is broken up. In the case of shipwreck it is often the first thing sought after, both as means of identifying the vessel and as an invaluable keepsake.

Bells can be quite famous, in some cases assuming almost mythical proportions. In the United Kingdom, Big Ben in London is the affectionate nickname for the bell of the clock in what is now known as Elizabeth Tower in the Palace of Westminster. The tower and Big Ben are representative of "everything British." United States has the Liberty Bell, a symbol of American independence, located in Philadelphia,

Pennsylvania, the birthplace of America and cradle of liberty.

Bells, like antiques, often don't take on any historical character or value, either monetary or symbolic, until they have aged—much like the artist who does not attain fame till long after death. This was true of *Queen Victoria*'s bell. At the date of the sinking, October 4, 1866, neither the ship nor her bell had any particular historical significance. A century would pass before the story behind the ship and her bell would attract attention, and only since then has the inherent symbolic value of *Queen Victoria*'s bell assumed historic proportions.

It was very strange that Captain Pouliot should remove the ship's bell from its mount at the foot of the mainmast even as *Queen Victoria* began her final plunge into the Atlantic. It would not have been an easy task. The bell weighed almost 100 pounds, and the extreme weather would have made it very difficult to get it aboard a lifeboat and transport it to *Ponvert*. It may well have been a conscious decision on the part of Captain Pouliot to remove the bell as a symbolic keepsake of his ship. He might also have entertained thoughts of its potential historic value as witness to the events of 1864 in Charlottetown and Quebec. We will never know. Nor do we know whether he, as the last person to abandon the steamer, took the ship's logbook with him. That would have been the norm, but it has never surfaced, if in fact he did.

What is known is that once all the survivors from *Queen Victoria* were safely aboard *Ponvert*, and sometime before they reached New York, Captain Pouliot presented *Queen Victoria*'s bell to Captain Rufus Allen as an expression of gratitude for saving the lives of her passengers and crew. It was quite a gesture, and one for which there is little precedent. Captain Allen was no doubt a modest man who would not have sought or expected anything for his service. It is an unwritten law of the sea that mariners come to the aid of ships in distress, in many instances to their own peril. Captain Pouliot would undoubtedly have done the same for Captain Allen and *Ponvert*.

That should have been the end of the story. In fact it was the beginning of another—the story of *Queen Victoria*'s bell.

Captain Allen remained at sea with *Ponvert* until 1873, when the brig was purchased and a different captain and crew put aboard. It did not bode well for *Ponvert*; she was wrecked in August of that same year. Rufus Allen had kept *Victoria*'s bell stored aboard *Ponvert* for the previous seven years. When the ship was sold, Allen took it ashore. Having no particular place to put the bell upon retiring in 1875, he gifted it to the school in Prospect Harbor. It was placed in a belfry and for the next seventy-five years it rang the children into school. Children and citizens alike knew nothing about the bell's history. Evidently Captain Allen didn't think it important enough to document for posterity. He kept whatever he knew of it to himself until his death in 1910.

In 1953, with the school and belfry in disrepair, a new school was built and the bell was presented to the Prospect Harbor Women's Club. For nearly a half-century it rested on a shelf in the Prospect Harbor Community House (the former Union Church), attracting only dust and minor curiosity as a souvenir of the area's nautical past. In or about 2003, the women's club conveyed it to the Town of Gouldsboro, which arranged to have it encased and put on display in the new Peninsula School. By this time, everyone in Gouldsboro and Prospect Harbor had become familiar with the bell's history.

Oddly enough, it was the subject of Canadian Confederation that brought the issue surrounding *Queen Victoria*'s bell to the forefront, both in Canada and United States. In the early 1960s, planning was under way in Canada to celebrate the centenary of Confederation. Committees were established in provinces across the country to plan special events to celebrate the first one hundred years of Canada's nationhood since July 1, 1867. It was a watershed time for the fledgling country with patriotic fervour very much in evidence in an otherwise staid populace.

Nova Scotia's representative on the centenary committee was Rear Admiral Hugh Pullen. He had entered the Royal Naval College of Canada at Esquimalt, British Columbia, in 1920. After spending two years with Canadian Pacific Steamship Company, he rejoined the Royal Canadian Navy in 1924. In 1944, during World War Two, he was decorated with the Order of the British Empire in recognition of his services while commanding a convoy escort group. Upon his retirement from the navy in 1960, he served as flag officer Atlantic Coast, Maritime Commander Atlantic, and Commander Atlantic Sub-Area (NATO), 1957–1960.

Rear Admiral Pullen was very active in retirement. Apart from being an accomplished author of maritime history, he was co-founder of the Maritime Museum of Canada, now the Maritime Museum of the Atlantic in Halifax. He made his home in Chester, Nova Scotia.

As a maritime historian Pullen became intrigued with the steamer *Queen Victoria* and the role she played in the story of Confederation.

The original bell from Queen Victoria, *on display at Peninsula School in Prospect Harbor, Maine.*

While working on plans for Canada's centenary, his keen interest in the *Queen Victoria* was met with scant information on the subject—in particular, the absence of any photograph of the ship. Undaunted, he determined to make every effort possible to redress this situation. In 1963, he wrote an open letter to the editor of the *Atlantic Advocate*, a regional magazine published in Fredericton, in which he broadcast his plea for assistance:

> Sir:
>
> *In 1864 a ship called* Queen Victoria *took the Fathers of Confederation from Quebec to Charlottetown, Halifax and St. John and back to Quebec. This voyage might well be called the prelude to Confederation, and certainly the Queen Victoria had a part to play in this great period in Canadian history.*
>
> *The ship was built by Robert Napier & Sons in Govan (Scotland) in 1856. She was an iron steamship of 300 horsepower with twin screw propellers (she had only one screw propeller). Her dimensions were as follows: length 173 feet; beam 30 feet; and depth in hold 16.5 feet. According to the shipping register at Quebec she had one deck and two masts, schooner rigged. She was built for Mr. Francis Baby of Quebec and had a sister ship called* Napoleon III. *The government held a mortgage on both ships and took them over in 1859.*

The Queen Victoria foundered on a passage from Havana on October 4, 1866. Her sister ship Napoleon III *was lost in a gale off the entrance to Little Glace Bay on October 18, 1890.*

In 1964 we will be celebrating the events which paved the way to confederation and the birth of the Dominion of Canada. A great deal is known about what took place in 1864, but apparently no one can say what the Queen Victoria *looked like. Here is a ship which should be known to every student of Canadian history, but like so many ships which have made their contribution to our progress, they have sailed away unknown, unrecorded and forgotten. A very thorough search has been made to try and find a picture or sketch or even plans of* Queen Victoria, *but so far without success. If any of your readers have any knowledge of this Canadian ship or know where I can get a picture of her, would they please get in touch with me?*

H. F. Pullen (Rear Admiral)
Big Hill, Chester, Nova Scotia

Little did he know then how his letter would start a chain reaction and eventually bring to light the fascinating story of *Queen Victoria*'s bell. One of the readers of the *Atlantic Advocate* was James E. Noonan, a long-

The model of Queen Victoria at Peninsula School in Prospect Harbor, Maine.

time resident of Prospect Harbor, Maine. Although he didn't have a photograph of the ship, he was sufficiently interested in the inquiry to contact Pullen, and over the course of the next three years, with Pullen's help, they located and pieced together the story of *Queen Victoria*'s bell.

In commenting on Rear Admiral Pullen's letter, in an interview in the *Ellsworth American* newspaper of December 14, 1966, Noonan, now deceased, said, "That's when I went to work digging. For three years I've dug." This newspaper article, written by John R. Wiggins, was titled "A Tale of Two Ships and a Bell." The caption that appeared beneath a photograph of the bell in the article reads, "Canada's Liberty Bell, Captain Allen's Prize." This was perhaps the first time the coined phrase "Canada's Liberty Bell" appeared in print. According to the local paper, his efforts were rewarded: "Research and correspondence proved that Prospect Harbor's bell once hung on the ship that Canadians are beginning to view with patriotic ardor."

The revelations about the bell's history, hidden away for the past century, engendered considerable interest in Canada, with not only Pullen but other government officials as Canada's hundredth birthday loomed just a few months ahead. It was not long before some of those Canadians involved in planning for the centennial descended upon Prospect Harbor to see the bell first-hand—and to inquire about the prospects for repatriating it to Canada.

However, the greater the interest expressed by Canadians for the bell, the more entrenched the Americans became in their desire to hold on to their now much-coveted bell. Cross-border diplomacy, or the lack of it, had begun. Little did those early participants know that the first shots in the "battle for the bell had been fired" in a contest of wills that would endure well into the next century.

In April of 1966, Noonan wrote to Pullen, the two having become quite well acquainted by then, to introduce him to a grandson of Captain Rufus Allen: Ralph Allen, then living in Santa Barbara, California. Through correspondence Pullen had confirmed that Ralph Allen had fallen heir to the silver tea service that his grandfather had managed to retain from the silverware taken from *Queen Victoria*.

In a letter dated May 19, 1966, from Allen to Pullen (whose mailing address reflected centennial year: PO Box 1967, Halifax, NS), Ralph Allen generously offered up the silver tea service: "Do you think that the Canadian Government would like the coffee pot and the teapot? When my wife and I are gone, there will be no one in our family for whom they have any sentimental attraction, and I would like to find a permanent home for them where they will be appreciated."

The gesture was most considerate. Rear Admiral Pullen responded without hesitation. Not surprisingly, Pullen suggested that the Maritime Museum in Halifax would be an appropriate place for these keepsakes. He introduced Allen to the director of the museum, and while it was some years before the final arrangements were consummated, in 1983 (the same year that Pullen passed away), the ornate two-piece set was formally donated to the Maritime Museum of the Atlantic, where it remains to this day. Pullen had succeeded in repatriating the only other known artifacts from the *Queen Victoria*—other than the bell. As for the bell, despite his best efforts, he failed.

It seems that the initial overtures made for the repatriation of *Queen Victoria*'s bell were all from private sources in Canada, with Rear Admiral Pullen—one of the chief architects of the centenary and Expo 67 in Montreal—being the catalyst. As revelations about the bell became more broadly spread, others joined with Pullen in an effort to repatriate the bell as part of the centennial celebrations.

They included marine historian and author Thomas Appleton, who at that time was employed by the Canada's Department of Transport. He, too, had considerable background knowledge of *Queen Victoria*. As well, Confederation Life, a Canadian insurance company, was compiling an art exhibit—Confederation Life's Gallery of Canadian History as part of Expo 67. It took an interest in *Queen Victoria* and her bell and numerous times approached the Prospect Harbor Women's Club about repatriating the bell through the club's PR manager Ian Murray. His last contact was a July 1969 letter he sent to the women's club, care of Mrs. Harriett Noonan (wife of James Noonan), enclosing two centennial portfolios of Canadian historical prints.

All these private initiatives were met with staunch resistance by residents of Prospect Harbor and Gouldsboro. It was all rather "cloak and dagger" stuff based on local rumours that the Canadians were bent on stealing the bell. From government agents disguised as insurance agents come to appraise the bell, to the tale of the occasion when members of the Royal Canadian Mounted Police "arrived in a helicopter bent on repossessing the relic." Thanks to the efforts of the women's club, the intruders "were repelled and sent packing." At this point the members of the women's club moved the bell into the town vault for safekeeping. They were having none of that—the "Minute women" of

Prospect Harbor carried the day and won the fray!

It seems there was some initial heavy-handedness—or at least the perception of it—on the part of a few Canadians, which may have resulted in the folks of Prospect Harbor becoming defensive and possessive about "their" bell. Once attention became focused on the bell as a result of the interest Canadians showed in it, the villagers were quick to assert their rightful claim to it. The Gouldsboro town manager described it as "symbolic of our maritime heritage and the courage, selflessness and seamanship of our forefathers that has been passed down through the generations where fishing here remains alive and well."

The Prospect Harbor Women's Club had refused permission to even loan the bell for the Canadian centennial, so Canada celebrated in 1967 without it. By this time, Pullen was fully occupied with oversight of the Atlantic Pavilion at Expo 67 in Montreal. He went on to pursue his other many and varied interests as a researcher and writer until his death in 1983. However, not before he had whetted the appetite of others who followed in his footsteps in what would become the "quest for the bell."

In Prospect Harbor the bell was very much the talk of town and soon voices, other than those in the women's club, were heard. Among them was Jonas Crane, a local writer and photographer. Late in 1967, while Canadians still celebrated their centennial, Crane wrote an article in a local newspaper titled "Canadians Want the Liberty Bell." This may have been among the first times that the phrase "Canada's Liberty Bell," referring to the ship's bell from the *Queen Victoria*, was coined. It has stuck ever since. In the piece, Crane recited some of the historical background surrounding ship and bell and the Canadians' interest in seeing it repatriated while noting the reluctance of the people of Prospect Harbor to part with "the beloved bell which was part of the colourful sailing days and the life of a native captain."

Shortly thereafter, Crane attained further notoriety on the subject when he authored yet another phrase, which has since become synonymous with the saga of the bell. In 1968, Crane wrote a feature for the *Imperial Oil Fleet News* titled "The Naughty Ladies of Prospect Harbour." It was obviously a follow-up to his earlier article, only this time he wrote about the "troubled conscience" of the Prospect Harbor Women's Club—"a group of ladies (now) feeling a little guilty when they think of Canada's big show" and their refusal to allow the loan of the bell for Expo 67."

Crane wrote that the club ladies had given a reluctant no to the

Canadian request, but "were not happy with their decision. They had the uncomfortable feeling that like naughty children they had made a selfish decision—one that was not a neighborly reply to their friends across the border." To quote one member, "It's like refusing to loan a cup of sugar to a neighbor who wants to make a birthday cake." Crane concluded his piece: "Hopefully history and Canadian opinion will deal kindly with the Prospect Harbor ladies for their single unneighborly act in a lifetime of good deeds. It might even come to pass that in time the naughty ladies will be able to look at their beloved bell without feeling guilty."

The first evidence of government intervention in Canada's quest for the bell occurred in 1971. In April of 1972, Mr. F. X. Houde, Canadian consul general in Boston, wrote to the women's club as a follow-up to a visit he had made to Prospect Harbor in 1971, "following a request by my Government that a further attempt be made to explain how grateful Canada would be if the bell which belonged to the SS *Queen Victoria* and which is now in the custody of the Women's Club could be donated to the Canadian people." The Canadian consul general's earlier visit had resulted in a failed attempt to persuade the women to relinquish the bell to Canada. In this letter, he offered to meet again with them to continue that discussion. The women's group could not have been feeling terribly guilty—they declined.

It did, however, motivate the women's club to further action in the political arena. They consulted the local United States senator Margaret Chase Smith and on behalf of the women's club wrote to the US Department of State to inquire as to whether Canadian officials had made any *formal* approach to that department concerning the bell. A letter in reply from the department dated April 28, 1972, noted: "To the best of our knowledge there has never been any official Canadian Government approach to the Department concerning the bell." The departmental spokesperson further remarked: "I believe it fair to say that, given this fact and the continuing sound relations we enjoy with Canada, the disposition of the bell should properly remain a matter for decision by its owners." Pretty heady stuff for the "naughty ladies" of Prospect Harbor. Now, further reassured, they vowed to maintain their stance on retention of the bell.

Interest in the bell soon spread beyond the tiny village of Prospect Harbor. In the spring of 1973, passions over the bell were further roused when the iconic *Yankee Magazine* published an article titled "Don't Give Up the Bell." After citing the history of the bell as unearthed by James Noonan's research, the author, Stephen N. McKinney, described the recent effort to retrieve the bell through the office of the Canadian consul and the resulting rebuff by the women's club. The ship's bell and the "naughty ladies" were fast becoming legendary.

McKinney concluded his article on a more a conciliatory note:

> There the matter stands today with the village bell—Canada's symbolic Liberty Bell—solidly in the possession of the ladies' club, which is adamant as ever about keeping it in the Community House. Some possibly wish there was a graceful way to back out and let the bell be on view to millions in Canada, but the people of Maine are legendary in their resistance to being pushed. So too are they legendary for their open-hearted generosity. Perhaps they will one day reconsider. One can easily envision the bell in the Canadian Parliament, with a plaque giving its colorful history and crediting the generous village of Prospect Harbor in furthering the bond of friendship between Canada and the United States. We must wait and see.

The following few years slipped by without incident, giving the illusion that Canadian interest in the bell had waned. This changed

Former school and church (now Women's Club) in Prospect Harbor, Maine, circa 1920.

dramatically in 1979, when Ian Trowell, a sculptor and writer from Mount Vernon, Prince Edward Island, got into the act. Trowell had been asked by the Fathers of Confederation Buildings Trust to determine the feasibility of creating a special Confederation exhibition for permanent display in the Confederation Centre. The Buildings Trust had overseen the construction of Confederation Centre of the Arts, a cultural centre dedicated to the visual and performing arts, located next to Province House in downtown Charlottetown. It is Canada's national memorial to the Fathers of Confederation and the Charlottetown Conference of 1864. The centre was officially opened by HRH Queen Elizabeth II on October 6, 1964, and designated a National Historic Site of Canada in 2003.

It was while researching material for such an exhibition that Trowell first learned about the SS *Queen Victoria* and the story surrounding her bell. It wasn't long before he made contact with the Prospect Harbor Women's Club with an impassioned plea for the return of the bell for this special exhibition. What followed was a litany of correspondence between Trowell and the ladies whose resolve to retain the bell remained unshaken.

"Naughty Ladies of Prospect Harbor" with the bell.

The Fathers of Confederation Exhibition, titled *The Iron Steamship Queen Victoria*, would eventually open in 1981, replete with a scale model of the ship constructed by Robert A. Nickerson of Bridgetown, Nova Scotia—but absent the ship's bell. Once again, the ladies of the Prospect Harbor Women's Club had denied Canadians their Liberty Bell.

Following the opening of the exhibition in what appears to have been Trowell's final communication with the club members on the subject, he remained optimistic that the ladies might yet change their minds. Using the occasion to send a catalogue of the exhibit that featured the ship, Trowell remarked, "Needless to say we would be delighted to amend the 'bell text' in upcoming printings to reveal our neighbors in Maine have acknowledged the importance of the bell to this exhibition by facilitating its return to Canada."

It was a vain hope. Trowell moved on, briefly stoking the embers of the move to repatriate the bell when he appeared as the subject of an article in the *Globe and Mail* under the banner "Historic Remnant Mired in U.S." This was essentially a lament over missed opportunity, the refusal by the "sweet old souls" of the Prospect Harbor Women's Club to turn over the bell, as well as a critique of "Canadian officialdom," which "doesn't seem to care about getting it back." In his parting comment on the subject, Trowell exhorted the Canadian government to take up the cause: "That's what the women of Prospect Harbor are waiting for—a clear indication from those who represent the people of Canada that we're sincere about wanting the 90 pound [sic] bell back."

This article did succeed in attracting the attention the Bell Collectors' Club of Ontario, which was a chapter of the parent organization, the American Bell Association. In a two-page letter dated August 18, 1984, and addressed to the women's club, the chairperson of the Ontario group cited the recent *Globe and Mail* article, and in support of Trowell's efforts encouraged the ladies to reconsider the gifting the bell to the Charlottetown exhibit. Nothing came of this.

The next effort to reclaim the bell also had its origins in Charlottetown. It was another anniversary with ties to Confederation. The 25th anniversary of the Confederation Centre of the Arts's opening was in 1989, which also coincided with the 125th anniversary of the Charlottetown Conference of 1864. Cause for celebration to be sure.

Sheila Daley and Mary Lou Hodge of the Gouldsboro Historical Society.

In 1987, Brian Anthony, executive director of the centre, assumed the role of chairman of a multi-party committee to plan and implement the celebrations marking these twin anniversaries in 1989. Anthony, like Ian Trowell before him, had no prior knowledge of the role SS *Queen Victoria* had played in the Confederation story, nor, until recently, the saga of the bell. He was quoted in the *Patriot*, a Charlottetown newspaper, as saying: "We were told of attempts that had been made before to get the bell of the *Victoria* back. I am a student of history but knew nothing of the history of the *Victoria* which had brought the Fathers of Confederation to this city. Not many really do."

So, stirred by sentiment and a new-found passion for *Queen Victoria's* bell and its role in the birth Canada, Anthony began correspondence with the Prospect Harbor Women's Club in yet another attempt to repatriate the bell. Beginning with a letter dated October 20, 1987, he wrote eloquently about the shared history of two neighbouring nations: "I appeal to you, your club members, and your fellow citizens from your State and your entire country to look favourably upon this request to return to Charlottetown and the people of Canada an artifact which is so important to the founding of our nation."

In the ensuing correspondence between Anthony and the club members, it very quickly became apparent that the original bell would not be relinquished to Charlottetown. Instead, there was talk of the possibility of a replica being made. In an odd moment of déjà vu and one of his more optimistic moments, when speaking about repatriation of the bell, Anthony quipped, "If they agree with us then perhaps we can strike a bell along with special plaques that express our gratitude to the United States for the bell's safe keeping." In the summer of 1988, the ladies advised Anthony that the club had turned the bell over to Gouldsboro and all further communications were to be directed to the town manager. The "naughty ladies of Prospect Harbor" had removed themselves from the fray—now any decision as to the ultimate disposition of the bell would rest with the town.

Anthony began negotiations with Gouldsboro only to learn that town officials, like the women's club before them, were intransigent in their resolve to keep their bell.

The anniversary planning committee, although forewarned, was undoubtedly surprised by the level of opposition and resistance put up in Prospect Harbor to the suggestion of repatriation. Anthony felt that one of the key elements in negotiations would be to convince the

Americans that the bell was more important to Canadians as "Canada's Liberty Bell" than it was to them. Retentionists in Prospect Harbor had previously expressed similar sentiments, arguing that no strong case had been put forward by the Canadian government. According to Anthony, in this bid, Confederation Centre had the support of all three levels of government as well as the involvement of the Canadian embassy in Washington. It was all to no avail.

In a final attempt to move the matter forward, Anthony wrote to John McKernan Jr., then governor of Maine, seeking his intervention in the Canadian quest for the bell. He also enlisted the support of Prince Edward Island premier Joseph Ghiz in writing the Maine governor. Governor McKernan replied to both Anthony and Ghiz, politely declining to intervene in the matter. It was effectively over—the 1989 celebratory events took place in Charlottetown without the *Queen Victoria*'s bell.

Things remained quiet for the next fifteen years. The Canadians withdrew, the issue was temporarily forgotten, and the bell was left unceremoniously "on the floor of the Gouldsboro town vault, under shelves crammed with folders and municipal documents, gathering dust."

In 2003, Canwest Global Communications Corporation, a major Canadian media company located in Winnipeg, Manitoba, launched its own probe into the history of *Queen Victoria*'s bell. That inquiry naturally took it to Prospect Harbor, which understandably was not anxious to reopen the old wounds from earlier skirmishes. Just when the villagers were probably thinking the matter about the bell had finally been laid to rest, it was now back in the glare of the media. The Gouldsboro town council grappled with the matter, seeking a way out of the impasse once and for all.

Two key figures then emerged, both of whom would play major roles in the implementation of a "magnanimous gesture" intended to placate the Canadians in their quest for *Queen Victoria*'s bell.

Ben Walter and his wife Soyna, who own and operate the Acadia Oceanside Meadows Inn at Prospect Harbor, proposed the idea of gifting a replica of the bell to Canada. Finding the expertise and a foundry capable of the task would normally be a considerable challenge. This case was quite the contrary: both the expertise and the foundry were available right in Prospect Harbor!

Richard Fisher had been handcrafting bells for five years when he and his wife moved to Maine in 1975. They built a small artisanal foundry in Prospect Harbor in 1982, specializing in the making of bronze bells, appropriately called US Bells. The small family business prospered to the extent that the original foundry was expanded a number of times. Richard Fisher was largely self-taught in the art of bronze casting, with much of what is turned out being custom work. He took on perhaps his greatest challenge in 2004 when asked by town officials in Gouldsboro if he would accept a commission to cast a bronze replica of *Queen Victoria*'s bell. He agreed.

This was no mean task. *Queen Victoria*'s bell was large and quite ornate. Fisher wanted to be sure to get it right. He was acutely aware that this commission was attracting more attention than usual. He refused to work under any deadline and instead took eighteen months to craft a replica. The finished product was a work of art, almost indistinguishable from the original other than colour—but it was nevertheless a replica. Meanwhile inn owner Walter spearheaded a fundraising campaign, which produced $2,500, more than enough to cover the actual cost. The surplus would be used to produce a plaque to describe the bell's historic significance.

Fisher felt considerable pressure as he worked on the casting. In October 2005, he completed the replica and just prior to turning it over to the town of Gouldsboro was quoted as saying, "I will feel good when it is finally settled, when the bell gets either here or there."

The replica was destined for "there," Charlottetown, Prince Edward Island. The original would remain "here" in Prospect Harbor, Maine. The problem was that even as late as the summer of 2006, Charlottetown was reportedly unaware of the offer for the bell. Sometime between June and August of that year arrangements were made with the officials in Charlottetown—it was from that city that interest had last been expressed in the bell—to accept a gift of the *Queen Victoria*'s bell replica.

Towards the latter part of August, Charlottetown mayor Clifford Lee visited Prospect Harbor, where he was presented with the homegrown replica from Gouldsboro by town manager Brad Vassey. According to Vassey, the residents recognized that the bell was important to Canada, and they intended to acknowledge that by "making an important gesture." At the formal ceremony, both bells, which had been mounted on a common belfry, were rung simultaneously. The "spirit of new friendship" was marked with the performance of both Canadian and American national anthems. Mayor Lee, one of only a few Canadians who were aware of the proceedings, expressed appreciation for the kind gesture by the people of Gouldsboro and left with the bell and a promise that it would be displayed prominently on the Charlottetown waterfront.

Mayor Lee made good on his promise. In mid-June of 2007, His Worship and a handful of people were present at Confederation Landing for the official unveiling of the replica bell. It was mounted in a wrought iron belfry, beside which Charlottetown town crier Bill MacFadyen stood to read his proclamation. It was a very quiet affair—not at all like the lavish social events that took place during that memorable week of the Charlottetown Conference back in 1864. Among those present was a small delegation from the United States, including Ben Walter, the Prospect Harbor community activist who spearheaded the replica project.

The Charlottetown mayor was happy with the outcome—the "compromise." He acknowledged that for the residents of Prospect Harbor it was important to have the original bell from *Queen Victoria* as a means of keeping alive the memory of Captain Rufus Allen and the area's seafaring heritage: "The bell is their claim to fame sort of thing. I think it was a very kind gesture on their part to offer to have a replica of the bell made and presented to the city of Charlottetown, which is honoured and indebted to the people of Maine for their very generous act of kindness."

After enjoying some of the many wonderful Island amenities, the American delegation returned home. It was a moment eerily reminiscent of 1864, when the Canadian delegates to the Charlottetown Conference returned home, believing that they had accomplished their mission. The Americans undoubtedly entertained similar thoughts as well as relief that finally the *Queen Victoria* bell issue had been put to rest. They and their fellow residents in Gouldsboro could now move on.

It wasn't to be.

CHAPTER 12

Canada's Liberty Bell

Americans are known to be very patriotic, Canadians perhaps less so, or at least they don't tend to show it as much. However, Confederation seems to be a subject for which Canadians rally around the flag. It was for the centennial in 1967, for Prince Edward Islanders celebrating the quasquicentennial and the 25th anniversary of the Confederation Centre of the Arts in 1989, and in 2017 as all Canadians joined in celebrating Canada's 150th anniversary—its sesquicentennial. These occasions pique feelings of national pride, and national symbols assume more importance than ever.

The United States has its Liberty Bell. It may have a crack in it, but it is original in every way. It is a symbol of nationhood appropriately displayed in Independence National Historical Park in Philadelphia, the cradle of American democracy. Canada too has its version of a Liberty Bell. The problem is most Canadians don't know of it, and even if they did, it is a replica—a very good replica—but not the original. There is and always will be a big difference, particularly where the original still exists. It is because of this difference that the *Queen Victoria* bell story continues to evolve, until recently causing deep divisions in Gouldsboro, Maine, which retains the original.

The next few years following the presentation of the replica bell passed quietly in Gouldsboro. The original bell remained on display in the Peninsula School in Gouldsboro. Early in 2014 it was once again the subject of further debate in the small Maine town.

The Canadian Museum of History is Canada's national museum of human history. Its roots stretch back to 1856, making it one of North America's oldest cultural institutions. It was formerly known as the Canadian Museum of Civilization. In 2013 its name was changed as well as its mandate, which is to enhance Canadians' knowledge and appreciation of "events, experiences, people and objects" which have shaped the country's history and identity. It is located in Gatineau, Quebec, across the Ottawa River from Parliament Hill in Ottawa.

With Canada soon to mark its 150th birthday in 2017, the museum embarked on compiling an exhibition that would introduce the topic and the country's path to nationhood. Titled *1867: Rebellion and Confederation*, the exhibition was curated by Jean-François Lozier. During the course of his research for the project, Lozier acquired materials relating to the steamer *Queen Victoria* and became aware of the existence of the original ship's bell in Prospect Harbor. It didn't take any time for him to conclude that the original bell could potentially be a focal point of his exhibit. To signify the bell's significance to Canada, Lozier—like Jonas Crane before him—likened it to the Liberty Bell, the symbol of American independence in Philadelphia: "It was a convenient label to use to get the message of the bell's importance across. Also it's an analogy we can use to mobilize more interest among Canadians.

Lozier sent a formal request for a loan of the bell to the Gouldsboro town council in December 2013. By the spring of 2014 the *Queen Victoria* bell was once again a common subject of conversation among the 1,700 residents of that small fishing community. Canadians, represented by the Canadian Museum of History, a federal Crown Corporation, were seeking a loan of the bell for the temporary exhibition, planned to open in November 2014. The issue was succinctly set out by the town manager in the Gouldsboro newsletter of April 2014: "At our recent meetings we have been discussing and considering the request of Jean-François Lozier, Curator, Canadian Museum of Civilization in Ottawa, Canada. The museum will be holding a major exhibition from November 2014 to September 2015. The celebration will mark the 150th anniversary of Canada's birth in 2017. The Canadian museum would like to borrow and display the original SS *Queen Victoria* Bell that is now safely displayed in Gouldsboro."

The newsletter was carefully crafted, outlining some of the earlier history around the bell in anticipation of a meeting of ratepayers to consider the request:

> While we understand the Canadian's desire to display a valuable piece of their heritage during this celebratory time, we are also very sensitive to the residents of Gouldsboro for whom the bell also holds rich meaning and embrace this gift that also marks a part of our history. It symbolizes our maritime heritage and the courage, selflessness and seamanship of our forefathers that has been passed down through the generations where fishing here remains alive and well. After careful consideration of this request, we decided

to bring the issue to our annual town meeting in June and ask residents if they wish to place the bell on loan to the museum.

Residents quickly mustered into two factions: those who favoured the loan and those who opposed it. It was a campaign fraught with emotion, and in some cases it pitted neighbour against neighbour, replete with fliers disseminated around town pitching arguments on both sides of the bell controversy.

As the town's annual meeting scheduled for June 11 approached, the war of words raged on. According to one local newspaper, "A rising chorus of acrimony over a famous ship's bell, which has been ringing through town the past few months, could reach a crescendo this week at the annual town meeting."

One of the town's five councillors, or selectmen, was Roger Bowen, a former president of the Milwaukee Natural History Museum. He had retired to Prospect Harbor just a few years earlier and was a vocal proponent of the loan: "I am in favour of lending the bell. It costs us nothing and in return it generates enormous goodwill." He acted as liaison between the Canadian museum and the town.

The contra-forces were exemplified by Beatrice Buckley, former president of the local historical society, who clearly did not share Bowen's view. She harboured a deep-seated fear that if loaned to the Canadian museum, the bell would never be returned. She hearkened back to "provocative demands" from Canadian authorities that the bell

Queen Victoria's *original (left) and replica bells, Prospect Harbor, Maine.*

be returned—a characterization others have disputed—as justification for her lack of trust in her northern neighbours. However, she may have succumbed to sheer emotion when she chose to personally attack Bowen as a recent "come from away" who didn't fully appreciate the bell's importance to the town's history: "We have a selectperson who wants fame and glory. He's behind the whole thing. We have a selectman who comes from out of state who doesn't give a hoot about our history and he doesn't see why the bell can't be loaned for nine months. I don't want to see them have it for as much as nine hours."

Bowen would have been forgiven had he chosen to respond in kind. Obviously that was not his style, and to his accuser(s) he simply responded: "I sometimes think people are accusing me of having a logic attack—and I plead guilty."

By this time there had been so much publicity and newspaper coverage that Gouldsboro residents were well aware of the historical background and importance to Canada of *Queen Victoria*'s bell. Before the all-important annual meeting, the local media had reported on the views of Canadian officials who felt it was no exaggeration to compare *Queen Victoria*'s bell to the Liberty Bell in terms of how both bells symbolize the births of their respective nations.

Mark O'Neill, president and CEO of the Canadian Museum of History, voiced support for the loan of the bell, saying it "played a major, major role in the history of Canada." In acknowledging their interest and pride in the bell, O'Neill assured Gouldsboro residents that the museum would fully insure the bell and guarantee its return in writing. He emphasized the critical importance the bell held for the exhibition, noting that there were not many material items that have historical significance to Canada.

Roger Bowen also emphasized the bell's importance to Canada. When he noted that Lozier had likened *Queen Victoria*'s bell to the American Liberty Bell, he said, "We can debate whether that's a fair analogy but that's the Canadian perspective. To them [Canadians] it's quite important."

Bowen wasn't at all concerned that the Canadians would keep the bell once it went across the border. In advocating the loan, he reminded residents that they were dealing with a "highly prestigious museum," likening it to the Smithsonian, which exhibited priceless treasures on loan every day. He reiterated their guarantee that the bell would be returned to Gouldsboro. "Besides," he said, "it's the neighbourly thing to do."

In the last days of the campaign, Buckley and another resident who opposed the loan spoke to a sixth-grade class at the Peninsula School about the bell's history. Later, while posing for a photograph beside the encased bell, an eighth grader joked that if the town loaned the bell to the museum it should charge the museum money and use the funds to build an indoor basketball court at the school. It was a prophetic comment, which would reverberate in the months ahead.

The annual meeting took place as scheduled on June 11. The hall was filled with approximately 120 residents all there for the vote on the loan. Following presentations on the subject, residents of Gouldsboro agreed with Bowen, and but for a few naysayers, the vast majority present voted in favour of the loan—at last. One of the few opposed, Beatrice Buckley, was predictably unhappy with the outcome and continued to blame the result on outsiders who don't know the history of the bell and still "don't give a hoot."

Roger Bowen spoke persuasively at the annual meeting about the benefits of the loan, which far outweighed any possible drawbacks. In counselling those present he stated, "Thousands upon thousands [of people] will go through the museum in Canada, their Smithsonian museum, and they will see the bell and they will see the little story written about it and Gouldsboro will suddenly go on the map of Canada."

Most everyone agreed and the town was directed to proceed with the loan for the exhibit which was originally planned to run November 11, 2014–September 9, 2015. For the first time in 150 years, *Queen Victoria*'s bell would return home, albeit briefly, and on loan. But for the unselfish

Prospect Harbor's Town Hall, Gouldsboro, Maine.

efforts of one American who had an affinity for Canada, and the occasional logic attack, it might not have happened.

Although the outcome of the annual meeting was never a foregone conclusion, in a prepared statement Mark O'Neill said that museum officials were pleased with the vote: "The loan of this important object stands as a testament to the long-standing friendship and collaboration between our two countries, and we are very grateful to the people of Gouldsboro for making it possible."

Soon after the exhibition opened, with *Queen Victoria*'s bell as one of the featured artifacts, Lozier wrote Gouldsboro council again—this time to ask for an extension in the loan to January 2016 because of the exhibit's popularity. According to Lozier, "The bell and its story in particular have been received with keen interest by the public."

Loan advocate Roger Bowen thought the request was reasonable, but when he took it to his selectmen colleagues he was immediately shot down. "I think it was sort of payback time," he said.

However, when museum officials offered to present Gouldsboro with a scale model of *Queen Victoria*, the selectmen had a change of heart. The extension was granted. After all, it hadn't cost the town anything.

Minutes from the Gouldsboro town meeting of January 14, 2016, noted that *Queen Victoria*'s bell would be returned from the Canadian Museum of History on January 27, 2016. The formal ceremony would be marked by an honorary luncheon to be attended by David Alward,

Roger Bowen and the model of Queen Victoria.

New England's consul general of Canada, and the museum curator. The now-famous bell was attracting the attention of more higher-ups in the Canadian political bureaucracy.

As it happened, Nicolas Gauvin, director of Business Partnerships and Information Management with the Canadian Museum of History, took the place of the museum curator on this occasion. David Alward, an American by birth, had just six months previously been appointed to the role of consul general. He had recently served one term as the thirty-second premier of the neighbouring Province of New Brunswick. Shortly after assuming his new office and in an official message from the consul general, Alward expressed pride in leading a dynamic team of dedicated public servants: "It is our mission to promote Canada's interests and to advance political and economic ties between Canada and New England."

From all accounts the ceremony was a pleasant affair. None of the acrimony that had divided the town eighteen months previously was displayed in the Peninsula School gymnasium on this day. The bell was back from Canada and with it came a beautiful scale model of *Queen Victoria*. The model, which the museum had commissioned for the recent exhibit, was presented to the town of Gouldsboro as a symbol of gratitude for the loan of the bell. It had been crafted with research and plans by Fred Werthman of Gananoque, Ontario, and the assistance of David Dean, a modeller in the employ of the Museum of Canadian History.

In presenting the model, Gauvin said, "It really represents the original and a lot of work was made to be able to reproduce it as ideally as possible." Commenting on the bell, he continued, "The bell we are returning to you today played an important part in Canadian independence. Thank you for lending us this important symbol of how our country came to be. This marks the first time in 150 years the bell has returned to Canada and we are very proud to have been able to include it in our exhibition."

If the consul general made any remarks, they did not appear to have been picked up by the media.

Roger Bowen was present and continued to encourage cooperation with Canadians over the bell. In addressing children present for the event, he told them it was important they know the bell's history and they be willing to share that history: "You will probably be asked someday by the Canadian Museum of History 'Can we borrow the bell again?' I encourage you to respond positively. It will be your decision to make."

He knew of what he spoke. Within a few short months the town would receive another request from Canadians for loan of the bell. The residents, not the schoolchildren, would have to decide—again.

Now both the bell and a large handcrafted model of *Queen Victoria* were in Gouldsboro's possession. It was the town manager's view that both should be kept in a "secure building," accessible to local residents and tourists alike. With no long-term plans for where to keep these precious artifacts, the town office would have to suffice for now. The import of his suggestion would ring out within a matter of days.

With fame comes responsibility. For more than fifty years, Canadians had demonstrated an ever-increasing interest in *Queen Victoria*'s bell. In that time, Gouldsboro's residents' awareness also increased regarding the bell's history and significance—to both Canadians and Americans alike. The bell, no longer just something that rang in a school belfry, had assumed a whole new meaning and value, something which Gouldsboro, as both owner and custodian, had to deal with sooner than anticipated.

The following month, in February of 2016, thieves broke into the Gouldsboro town office, where both the bell and the ship model had been stored following the January ceremony. The burglars forced their way in through the back door and broke the door to the vault before making off with police handguns, drugs, and money. They couldn't have been following the saga of *Queen Victoria*'s bell, for they left it and the ship model alone.

"The bell is fine," said relieved town manager Bryan Kaenrath.

It was a poignant reminder of the comments Kaenrath had voiced just a few weeks before when speaking about the bell and model and the need for a "secure building." Clearly the town office was not that building. The town residents, not to mention all Canadians, were left to ponder what if.

For the present, at least, it was something for Gouldsboro to address. The town manager advised that there would be some security upgrades at the town office: "We are going to be looking at building security. With a case like this we have to make some changes."

A clear understanding of the great responsibility, and because of it a greater standard of care, is what is now required. Next time—if there is a next time—the town and all those who cherish *Queen Victoria*'s irreplaceable bell, may not be so lucky. Maybe an independence hall is needed, or perhaps the secure facility of the sort offered by the Canadian Museum of History?

Roger Bowen was formerly in the museum business, so he probably had a sense of the veracity of his prediction when he suggested to the schoolchildren of Gouldsboro that they might anticipate future requests from Canadians for the loan of the bell. And his prediction soon came to fruition.

In the summer of 2016, curator Jean-François Lozier was back in Gouldsboro seeking another loan of the bell, only this time on behalf of another Canadian museum. The exhibit for the Canadian Museum of History promoting Canada's 150th anniversary had been crafted with the intention of being portable, and it was about to be on the move.

The Canadian Museum for Human Rights, another of Canada's national museums, is located in Winnipeg, Manitoba. This one, just opened in 2014, was the first new national museum to be built since Confederation in 1967. It was the brain-child of Israel "Izzy" Asper, a Canadian lawyer, politician, and founder of the now defunct media conglomerate Canwest Global Communications, which had launched its own inquiry into the *Queen Victoria* story back in 2003. According to the enabling legislation by which it was established, the purpose of the museum is "to explore the subject of human rights, with special but not exclusive reference to Canada in order to enhance the public's understanding of human rights, to promote respect for others and to encourage reflection and dialogue."

The Canadian Museum for Human Rights wanted its own exhibit to mark Canada's sesquicentennial in 2017. To that end, it created an adaptation of *1867: Rebellion and Confederation* with an increased emphasis on "efforts that helped achieve some of our [Canadian] fundamental freedoms and rights." Working closely with its counterpart the Canadian Museum of History, and believing the bell to be an integral element for its own exhibit, this museum also sought a similar loan arrangement. Jean-François Lozier, a now familiar face in Gouldsboro, acted as liaison and negotiator on behalf of the Canadian Museum of Human Rights.

Lozier was in Gouldsboro in July 2016 to talk about the new loan request. He had also been invited to speak at the Dorcas Library about the history of the bell. Shortly after his visit, it was reported in the local press that "*Queen Victoria*'s bell would be on the move again." This time, however, the terms would be different. The town must have picked up on the suggestion by the Peninsula School eighth grader, who a year earlier had jokingly suggested that the town should charge rent for any future loan of the bell. Evidently the town council was of the same mind, and seeing that there was money now to be made, the terms were specified and agreed to by the Museum of Human Rights—all in short order and without any divisive debate within the community. Money talks.

The September 2016 Gouldsboro newsletter made brief reference to the latest loan arrangement. It was announced with neither fanfare nor derision: "The *Queen Victoria* bell will once again be travelling. The Canadian Museum for Human Rights will have the bell on loan for the upcoming winter in an exhibit similar to the previous one used by the Canadian Museum of History. The town of Gouldsboro will be charging a rental fee of $2000.00 per month for the loan."

The bell was crated up and transported all at the expense of the Winnipeg museum in time for the exhibit opening on December 13, 2016. In a relatively short period of time, *Queen Victoria*'s bell seemed to have appreciated greatly in value. As part of the deal, the Winnipeg museum agreed to arrange for and carry a $1 million insurance policy on the bell. The ship model did not accompany the bell. Maybe the rent would have been prohibitive. Or possibly neither the museum nor the town saw any particular significance to the ship. Perhaps in time, the ship model, like the bell, will assume more importance. Now might be a good time for the Canadian Museum of History to attempt to take it back.

The Winnipeg exhibition was to run for approximately six months with the bell to be returned to Gouldsboro no later than May 2017. It was a win-win deal for the town. A single month's rent would cover the cost of the bell replica presented as a compromise to Charlottetown back in 2007, and the balance of approximately $10,000 USD would, if at least one of the local students had their way, kick-start the school basketball court.

According to the town manager, the rental income from the bell would be donated to local organizations such as Beatrice Buckley's Gouldsboro Historical Society: "It won't just go to the general fund. It will go to local organizations that could really use the money."

Canadians were now paying to borrow Canada's Liberty Bell—symbolic of nationhood—and in the process helping to finance the preservation of Gouldsboro's local maritime history. Good deal for Gouldsboro, not so good for Canada.

EPILOGUE

For Whom the Bell Tolls

The steamer *Queen Victoria* played a pivotal role in events leading to Confederation of Canada in 1867. Although the notion may not have been fully appreciated in 1866 at the time of her sinking, it is now commonly accepted by both political and maritime historians.

The ship really had two lives. The first marked that period from construction in 1855 by the renowned marine engineer and shipbuilder Robert Napier and her fascinating service record as a workboat and royal yacht, ending with her sinking while under charter as part of a new commercial venture. The second segment of the *Queen Victoria* story begins from the moment she sinks and Captain Paul Pouliot is the last to abandon the doomed steamer with the ship's bell in hand. It is through *Queen Victoria*'s bell that the history of the ship is ultimately brought to light.

Queen Victoria was designed and constructed in arguably the finest shipyard of the time as a tug tender. The Robert Napier & Sons yard represented the "leading edge" of iron-hull steamship building in the mid-nineteenth century. *Queen Victoria* was technologically advanced and of a superior class when delivered to François Baby in 1856. She and her sister ship, *Napoleon III*, worked together in the service of Trinity House of Quebec in protecting shipping and perfecting navigation on the St. Lawrence River. Together they formed the backbone of what would become the Canadian Coast Guard.

Those laurels may have been enough in their own right to preserve a place for *Queen Victoria* in Canadian maritime history. However, she was destined for something more. For a decade she fulfilled diverse roles and hosted and transported representatives of the Crown as well as royalty. She and her crew, led by Captain Paul Pouliot, were able to make the transition from work boat to regal flagship with comparative ease and aplomb. Captain Pouliot was highly regarded both as a master and a diplomat. Those occasions served as training for the voyage that would indelibly engrain the name of this ship in the annals of Canadian nationhood, when she became both transport and a floating hotel for Canada's future Fathers of Confederation.

Queen Victoria's future was somewhat uncertain when she sunk during a hurricane. Even then, however, she was transformational. At the time of her loss she was engaged in a charter as part of an experimental voyage intended to foster increased trade opportunities between Canada and Cuba. Her sinking was a loss, but nothing out of the ordinary at a time when ships of all makes and sizes regularly succumbed to the forces of nature.

It was very fortunate, even miraculous perhaps, that Captain Rufus Allen and his stout brig *Ponvert* arrived on the scene and successfully rescued *Queen Victoria*'s passengers and crew. Most assuredly, they expressed their gratitude to Captain Allen by gifting to him silverware and the ship's bell. However heroic Captain Allen's actions may have been, they were neither unusual nor extraordinary for those who made their life at sea. Rescue efforts such as his to "those in peril on the sea" were commonplace as part of the unwritten "law of the sea." What was extraordinary in this case was the removal and gifting of *Queen Victoria*'s bell.

Today, the question lingers as to whether Captain Pouliot had any right to give the ship's bell to Captain Allen. The ship and the bell were the property of the Canadian government, and some might argue remain so to this day. However this aside is beyond the scope of this book and is best left to legal scholars and maritime law specialists. There was talk in the 1980s of possibly trying to raise the wreck, an eventuality which might spark that debate.

The author with Captain Allen's headstone in Prospect Harbor, Maine.

What is quite clear is that *Queen Victoria*'s bell remained in almost total obscurity for nearly a century. It was not until the mid-1960s, thanks to the efforts of Rear Admiral Pullen—aided by Prospect Harbor resident James Noonan—that the story about the ship and its bell began to surface. As the story evolved and became public, so did the interest of some Canadians in what would soon be referred to as Canada's Liberty Bell. By this time, the folks in Prospect Harbor and Gouldsboro had come to realize that the bell, which until then had meant virtually nothing, had now taken on special meaning and value in respect to its maritime heritage. One bell and now two competing interests.

The author with Queen Victoria's *replica bell in Charlottetown, PEI.*

The events that subsequently unfolded were in many ways unplanned, uncoordinated, and unfortunate. According to stories told in and around Gouldsboro, forays were made to Prospect Harbor by individuals or small groups from north of the border, seeking the return of the bell to Canada. There doesn't appear to be any documentation to substantiate some of the more colourful accounts, but the end result appears to have been a hardening of positions on both sides of the campaign for *Queen Victoria*'s bell.

In retrospect it is not difficult to understand how and why things unravelled as they did. The playing field was not even. Gouldsboro had possession of the bell, and the Prospect Harbor Women's Club was a staunch foe. The 1,700 residents of Gouldsboro became increasingly protective of the bell as symbolic of their maritime heritage. They represented a unified force. There was no such cohesiveness in Canada. To that point, in Canada interest in the bell had been expressed by only a few individuals. Canada as a country had yet to learn about both the ship and its bell. One Prospect Harbor resident suggested that until the Canadian government put forth a credible claim, the bell should remain where it is. That was not entirely unreasonable, and perhaps it was what should have transpired. The problem was, and remains, that to garner support, there must first be widespread knowledge and

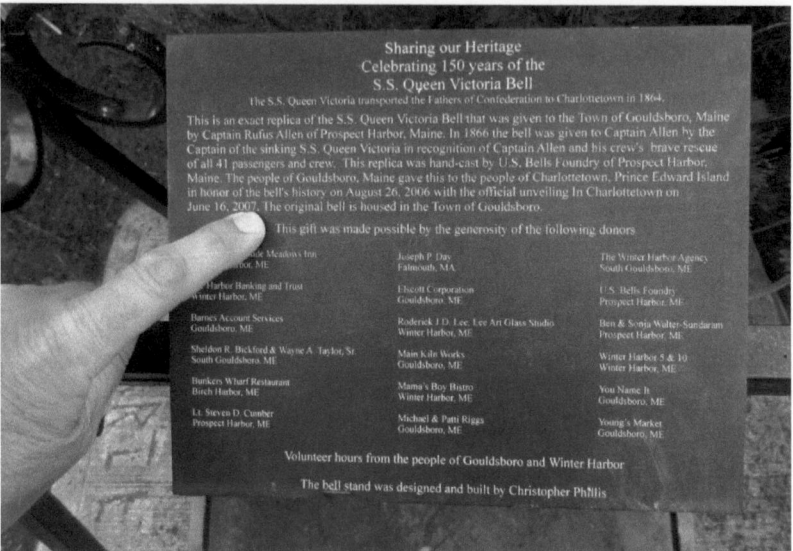

The plaque accompanying Queen Victoria's *replica bell in Charlottetown, PEI.*

understanding of the subject. In fact, to this day, the story is not well known by Canadians.

It is true that a replica of the original bell is now on display in Confederation Landing in Charlottetown. The reproduction is a fine piece of workmanship, but is a replica. And the replica was a fine gesture by the people of Gouldsboro, although it was intended as a compromise, a way out of the ongoing battle for the bell. The Confederation Centre had made an unsuccessful attempt to repatriate the bell to Charlottetown in the 1980s. Its donors (eighteen individuals and businesses in Gouldsboro whose names are etched in the plaque that accompanies the bell) may have intended it to be a gift to Canadians, but in fact it was an arrangement made and a token accepted in a quiet ceremony by civic officials in Charlottetown entirely unbeknownst to Canadians. Characteristically, Prince Edward Island had again chosen to "go on its own," this time to unilaterally accept the terms of surrender to Canada's claim to the original bell. It was an arrangement that was neither represented to nor ratified by Canadians.

Recent events give further support to the inevitability that the original bell, particularly once Canadians become aware of its symbolism, will remain the focus of Canadian historians, cultural institutions, and residents. It is already happening.

By 2015, Gouldsboro residents were quite cognizant of the bell's significance to Canada. Any thoughts of repatriating the bell at this time were quickly shelved when it became obvious just how possessive the local residents had become. A loan seemed to be the path of least resistance; however, it was another missed opportunity for Canada to assert its claim to the bell. If anything, the loan further emboldened and strengthened the town's hold on the bell.

It seems Canadians were not about to be outdone when it came to generous gestures. The bell was returned after the Ottawa exhibit and to show their appreciation for the loan, the museum presented the Maine town with a fine scale model of *Queen Victoria*. Now the town of Gouldsboro had the bell and a model of the ship—a virtual museum— artifacts to explain *local* history to both residents and tourists. The Canadian Museum of History—Canada's leading museum—had neither to demonstrate these symbols of a nation, its own Confederation

More recently, the enterprising people of Gouldsboro have come up with a solution to the ever-increasing Canadian demand for the original bell. And another Canadian cultural institution has helped to foster the latest scheme: renting out the bell. A solution to continued requests for loan of the bell was required if for no other reason than to placate townspeople who had tired of the bell issue. The answer was "clear as a bell"; the words of the eighth grader rang in the ears of the town council. The town agreed to lease the bell. Gouldsboro could reap financial reward from its prized artifact, a proposition that had obvious appeal to its citizens. The Canadian Museum of Human Rights bought into this scheme and may have helped to set a precedent, which undoubtedly Gouldsboro hopes will continue. Perhaps they will soon thank Canadians for building the new school basketball court—and more.

Queen Victoria's bell has seemingly appreciated tremendously in value since Canadians have discovered its existence. The Museum of Human Rights was obligated to secure insurance coverage of $1 million on the bell during the term of its lease. Although as the inherent value escalates, so too does the onus on the custodians to provide for its security. Gouldsboro, like it or not, now has a fiduciary duty towards Canada to "preserve and protect," which it didn't have before the bell came into such prominence.

Although it was never described as such, around home while growing up there was a sort of unwritten eleventh commandment of "always try to do what is right." Until answered someday, the question will always remain: what is the right thing for Gouldsboro to do with its bell? If one were to suggest that the original should be repatriated to Canada, would one be accused of having a logic attack? If so, I and countless other Canadians would plead guilty.

So, this begs the question: what if the shoe was on the other foot? What if a small fishing community in Nova Scotia, Canada, with every bit as much connection to a seafaring past as Gouldsboro came into possession, under similar circumstances of the equivalent of America's Liberty Bell? Americans would most likely clamour loudly for it. The same competing interests of local heritage versus national symbolism would clash. Maybe Gouldsboro might yet set the proper standard in case ever such a situation should arise.

What Canadians may lack, and need, is a little more of Americans' passion for their own history as well as political will. As more Canadians learn about *Queen Victoria*'s bell, hopefully it will take on increased importance to an informed population. Canada is short on symbols. Every nation needs one. Canada's Liberty Bell could be such a symbol.

The last chapter in the story of the steamer *Queen Victoria* and her bell has not been written. Gouldsboro may yet have to grapple with the question of what is the right thing to do. Maybe a new generation in Gouldsboro, brought up to understand the history and relevance of the bell to both Canada and that Maine fishing and seafaring community, will look more favourably upon repatriation to Canada and ultimately make that decision.

Acknowledgments

A book, particularly a work of non-fiction, is seldom written in isolation. In my experience, one of the most rewarding aspects of writing is the people you meet along the way. This has proven to be the case in the research and writing of this book. Many people are to be thanked for their insight and guidance in helping to bring this story to fruition.

First and foremost, I am indebted to two masters of the sea, one who is well known to me and the other who I unfortunately never had the good fortune to meet. Captain Ian McNaught who served as the last master of the Cunard Line flagship *Queen Elizabeth 2*, apart from being a good friend, graciously agreed to compose the foreword to this narrative. This is most appropriate given his current role as deputy master of Trinity House UK, one of Britain's oldest and most venerable institutions. The other is Rear Admiral Hugh Francis Pullen. After a distinguished career with the Canadian Navy, he became a well-known maritime historian and author. He was the inspiration for this book.

The *Queen Victoria* was home-ported in Quebec City, and her workplace was the St. Lawrence River, with her travels taking her throughout the Gulf of St. Lawrence and the Maritime provinces. It is not surprising then that sources accessed from within this geographical area produced a wealth of information that contributed considerably to this effort. In Charlottetown, Prince Edward Island, my thanks to Pan Wendt, curator of Confederation Centre Art Gallery; and Paige Matthie, registrar, for their kindness in sharing artwork to supplement this story. Through their efforts I was also introduced to H. T. Holman, former Prince Edward Island principal archivist, who was helpful in suggesting references regarding *Queen Victoria*. Ian Cheverie, guest services manager for the Great George, Charlottetown's boutique hotel, was kind enough to provide me with information about this historic hostelry.

In Nova Scotia, Roger Marsters, curator of maritime history at the Maritime Museum of the Atlantic, was most helpful in providing reference materials about the Confederate raider *Tallahassee*. It is always a pleasure to spend time at the Nova Scotia Archives, a veritable treasure-trove of historical information. The staff, as always, gave freely of their time with my research, particularly my good friend and archivist cum laude Virginia Clark.

In *la belle province* of Quebec I wish to express my appreciation to a number of people. Alain Franck, curator at the Maritime Museum of Quebec situated on the St. Lawrence River at L'Islet-sur-Mer, was very obliging in sourcing reference materials from that site. So, too, were Peter Gagne, curator, and Ariane Fréchette at the Museum of Civilization in Quebec City. These folks were introduced to me by my friend Suzanne Fortier, who so willingly gave of her time and effort to my research. At the Morrin Center in Old Quebec, Deborah van der Linde was very helpful in responding to my request for reference materials in that repository.

In Ontario, I wish to thank Jean-François Lozier with the Department of History at the University of Ottawa for sharing his own experience with the saga of *Queen Victoria*. Through him, I also came into contact with Fred Werthman in Gananoque. Fred's enthusiasm for the subject and the particulars he shared regarding the vessel's specifications were invaluable and edifying.

My research took me into the United States, where in Prospect Harbor, Maine, I had the pleasure of meeting two very fine ladies, Sheila Daley and Mary Lou Hodge with the Gouldsboro Historical Society. Sheila, as lead spokesperson, helped provide full access to the historical records of the society housed within a quaint church in a rural setting not far from town. For me, they are and will always remain "the lovely ladies" of Prospect Harbor. Equally charitable with his time and interest was Roger Bowen, a village councillor who very graciously made himself available to meet over lunch one day and share his own experience with the *Queen Victoria*'s bell. Finally, while in Prospect Harbor, I was welcomed into the home of Mrs. Edesse Fox, whose warm hospitality and shared insights into the saga of the bell were both entertaining and enlightening.

I would be quite remiss if I didn't acknowledge my wife, Judith, for her patience and encouragement.

Not to be overlooked are the good people at Nimbus Publishing in Halifax, including general manager Terrilee Bulger, managing editor Whitney Moran, and editor Elaine McCluskey for their commitment to seeing this project through. The "team" also included freelance editor Paula Sarson, who worked with the author in producing the final product. Paula's quiet professionalism, sensitivity, and overseeing made editing this work a most enjoyable experience.

It has been quite a voyage. Sincere thanks to all.

Appendix 1

Short biographies for the Fathers of Confederation

Twenty-three delegates attended the Charlottetown Conference from September 1–9, 1864: five representatives from each of the Maritime provinces of Nova Scotia, New Brunswick, and Prince Edward Island; and eight from Canada (Canadian ministry), including four from the provinces of Ontario and Quebec, respectively. (*Note:* The Act of Union of 1841 created the United Province of Canada, combining what was Upper Canada (Ontario) with Lower Canada (Quebec). They were subsequently referred to as Canada West and Canada East, and following Confederation in 1867, would revert back to simply Ontario and Quebec. To avoid confusion, I have chosen to say simply "Ontario" and "Quebec" for this appendix.)

ONTARIO

Sir John A. Macdonald: Born in Glasgow, Scotland, on January 11, 1815, and brought up in Kingston, Ontario, where he moved with his parents at the age of five. Was a lawyer turned politician, first elected to the legislature of the Province of Canada in 1844, became premier in 1857 and first prime minister of Canada upon Confederation in 1867. He served in that capacity for a total of nineteen years, 1867–1873 and 1878–1891.

Sir Alexander Campbell: Born in Hedon, England, on March 9, 1822, and settled with his family in Kingston, Ontario, in 1836. Became a lawyer and partner with John A. Macdonald, which brought about a political alliance between these two men. Elected to the Legislative Council of Province of Canada in 1858 and 1864 and served as the last commissioner of Crown lands 1864–1867 and as the sixth lieutenant-governor of Ontario 1887–1892.

William McDougall: Born in York (Toronto) on January 25, 1822. Worked as a lawyer, journalist, and newspaper owner and politician. He was elected to the legislative assembly of Ontario in 1858 and served as commissioner of Crown lands and provincial secretary. Post-Confederation he was Minister of Public Works 1867–1869.

George Brown: Born at Alloa, Clackmannanshire, Scotland, on November 29, 1818. Worked as a journalist and politician. He established the *Toronto Globe* newspaper in 1844, which under his ownership became the most powerful newspaper in British North America. He was very briefly premier of the Province of Canada in 1858. Brown joined John A. Macdonald and George Cartier in Cabinet as president of the council during the Great Coalition of June 1864. He played a major role in securing national unity.

QUEBEC

George-Étienne Cartier: Born September 6, 1814, at Saint-Antoine-sur-Richelieu, Lower Canada (Quebec). Worked as a lawyer and politician. Elected to the legislative assembly of Province of Canada in 1848 and created the Great Coalition with friends Macdonald and Brown in 1864. Served as Minister of Militia and Defence upon creation of the Dominion of Canada in 1867.

Sir Alexander Tilloch Galt: Born September 6, 1817, in Chelsea (London), England. Was a businessman, politician, author, and diplomat. Of Scottish descent, he was a first cousin of Sir Hugh Allan of Montreal, founder of the Allan Line of steamships. Was inspector-general of the Province of Canada and in 1880 became the first Canadian high commissioner in London.

Sir Hector-Louis Langevin: Born August 25, 1826, at Quebec, with deep roots in that province. Worked as a lawyer, journalist, and politician. Was mayor of Quebec City 1858–1861. As a member of the Conservative Party in Lower Canada, he held various positions in Cabinet both before and after Confederation.

Thomas D'Arcy McGee: Born April 13, 1825, in Carlingford, Republic of Ireland. Spent his formative years in Ireland where his father, James, worked in the Coast Guard Service. Worked as a journalist, poet, and politician. Came to North America in 1842, living first in United States before moving to Montreal in 1857. The following year he was elected to the legislative assembly of Canada and worked for the creation of an independent Canada. He was assassinated in Ottawa, Ontario, by Patrick J. Whelan, a Fenian sympathizer, on April 7, 1868.

NOVA SCOTIA

Sir Charles Tupper: Born near Amherst on July 2, 1821. Was a doctor and politician. Served as provincial secretary during tenure of James William Johnson as premier of Nova Scotia and then became premier himself in 1864. Resigned as premier of Nova Scotia after Confederation to take up different federal Cabinet posts under Prime Minister John A. Macdonald. Was second to be appointed Canadian high commissioner to the United Kingdom and served very briefly as sixth prime minister of Canada in 1896.

Robert Barry Dickey: Born in Amherst on November 10, 1811. Worked as a lawyer and politician. Served in the Nova Scotia Legislative Council from 1858 until 1867, when he was appointed to the Canadian Senate.

William Alexander Henry: Born in Halifax on December 30, 1816. Worked as a lawyer, politician, and judge. Served as a Cabinet minister under both Conservative and Liberal governments in Nova Scotia and was Attorney General in 1864. Was one of the first appointed to the new Supreme Court of Canada in 1875.

Jonathan McCully: Born around Maccan, Nova Scotia, on July 25, 1809. Was a lawyer, journalist, senator, and judge. He wrote frequently espousing his political beliefs in two Halifax newspapers, *Acadian Recorder* and *Halifax Morning Chronicle*. He held various offices while serving in the Nova Scotia Legislative Council and following Confederation was appointed to the Senate of Canada.

Sir Adams George Archibald: Born May 3, 1814, in Truro, Nova Scotia. Worked as a politician and judge. Elected to the Nova Scotia legislature in 1851, appointed Solicitor General in 1856, and Attorney General in 1860. Post-Confederation he was appointed Secretary of State for the provinces in the Cabinet of John A. Macdonald. He served as lieutenant-governor of Nova Scotia 1873–1883.

NEW BRUNSWICK

Edward Barron Chandler: Born at Amherst, Nova Scotia, on August 22, 1800. Was a lawyer, politician, and judge. Served as a member of the New Brunswick Legislative Council and as the fifth lieutenant-governor of New Brunswick 1878–1880.

John Hamilton Gray: Born in St. George, Bermuda, in 1814. Worked as a lawyer, politician, and judge. He was premier of New Brunswick 1856–1857. Post-Confederation he served briefly in the House of Commons before being appointed judge of the Supreme Court of British Columbia. He died in Victoria, British Columbia, in 1889 and is the only Father of Confederation buried west of Ontario.

John Mercer Johnston: Born in Liverpool, England, in October 1818. Was a lawyer and politician. Moved to Chatham, New Brunswick, in 1821. He held various positions in the New Brunswick assembly and was Attorney General 1862–1865. Post-Confederation he was successful in his bid for a seat in the Federal House of Commons.

William Henry Steeves: Born May 20, 1814, at Hillsborough, New Brunswick. Was a merchant, lumberman, and politician. A leader in the financial community in Saint John, he was first elected to New Brunswick's House of Assembly in 1846. He later served as Surveyor General and variously chairman and commissioner of public works. He was appointed to the Canadian Senate in 1867.

Sir Samuel Leonard Tilley: Born May 8, 1818, at Gagetown, New Brunswick. Worked as a druggist and politician. He was a certified pharmacist who went into partnership with a cousin, Thomas W. Peters. Staunch advocate of the temperance movement. First elected to the New Brunswick assembly in 1850 and later became provincial secretary. He was premier of New Brunswick 1861–1865. Post-Confederation he held various positions in the federal government and served twice as New Brunswick's lieutenant-governor in 1873 and 1885.

PRINCE EDWARD ISLAND

William Henry Pope: Born May 29, 1825, at Bedeque, Prince Edward Island. Worked as a lawyer, politician, and judge. Editor of *The Islander* newspaper. Was named colonial secretary for the province in 1859 and entered politics in 1863 but left Cabinet in 1864 when the Island government rejected Confederation outright. He was appointed county court judge after his brother James Colledge Pope became premier.

George Coles: Born in Prince Edward Island, September 20, 1810. Worked as a farmer, merchant, brewer, distiller, and politician. He first entered politics in 1841. Following the granting of responsible government in 1851, he became the Island's first premier and served again in that capacity 1867–1869.

John Hamilton Gray: Born June 14, 1811, at Charlottetown. Was a soldier and politician. Son of a Loyalist father, Gray initially chose a military career before entering provincial politics. He was a Conservative member of the legislative assembly and premier of Prince Edward Island 1863–1865. He was chairman of the Charlottetown Conference and supported the entry of the Island into Confederation. When the Island rejected that scheme, he left politics, turning the government over to James Colledge Pope.

Andrew Archibald Macdonald: Born February 14, 1829, at Brudenell Point, Prince Edward Island. Was a merchant and politician. Elected to Legislative Assembly of Prince Edward Island 1853–1858. Appointed postmaster general in 1873. Became the Island's fourth lieutenant-governor in 1884. At the age of thirty-five he was the youngest of the Maritime delegates at the Charlottetown Conference.

Edward Palmer: Born at Charlottetown, September 1, 1809. Worked as a lawyer, land agent, politician, and judge. Was leader of the minority Tory party and when it took office was made Attorney General in 1853. He opposed Maritime Union as well as Confederation, which he demonstrated at the Quebec Conference where he was described as a "thorn in the flesh of those committed to Union." In 1873 when PEI did join Confederation, Palmer was made judge of Queen's County court.

There were thirty-three delegates at the Quebec Conference from October 12–27, 1864. All twenty-three delegates who participated at Charlottetown attended. As well, the provinces of Ontario, Quebec, New Brunswick, and Prince Edward Island each added two more delegates to their rosters. Newfoundland, with two delegates, participated for the first time.

ONTARIO

Sir John Alexander Macdonald
Sir Alexander Campbell
William MacDougall
George Brown

James Cockburn: Born February 13, 1819, at Berwick-upon-Tweed, England. Worked as a lawyer, businessman, and politician. Elected to the Province of Canada's Legislative Assembly in 1861. Was a supporter of Confederation, after which he was elected to the new House of Commons. He was made first Speaker of the House of Commons 1867–1874.

Sir Oliver Mowat: Born at Kingston, Ontario, July 22, 1820. Worked as a lawyer, politician, and judge. He articled in the law office of John A. Macdonald. Member of the legislative council for Province of Ontario 1858–1864, during which time he served as provincial secretary and postmaster general. He became the third premier of Ontario, an office he held for twenty-four years 1872–1896, after which he was appointed eighth lieutenant-governor of Ontario.

QUEBEC

Sir George Étienne Cartier
Sir Alexander Tilloch Galt
Sir Hector-Louis Langevin
Thomas D'Arcy McGee

Jean-Charles Chapais: Born at Rivière-Ouelle on December 2, 1811. Was a businessman and politician. He entered politics in 1851 and was elected to the legislative assembly of Quebec, serving a total of five terms representing Kamouraska. He was Minister of Public Works in the Great Coalition 1864–1867. After Confederation he became Minister of Agriculture and receiver general for Canada. He became a senator in 1868.

Sir Etienne Paschal Taché: Born September 5, 1795, at Saint-Thomas (Montmagny), Quebec. Was a doctor and politician. Elected to the legislative assembly in Quebec in 1841, holding numerous posts and serving briefly as premier of Canada. He was an ardent supporter of the British Crown. He presided over the Quebec Conference. He was credited with coining the phrase and provincial motto of Quebec: *"Je me souviens"* (I remember).

NOVA SCOTIA

Sir Charles Tupper
Robert Barry Dickey
William Alexander Henry
Jonathan McCulley
Sir Adams George Archibald

NEW BRUNSWICK

John Mercer Johnston
Sir Samuel Leonard Tilley

Charles Fisher: Born 1808 at Fredericton, New Brunswick. Worked as a lawyer, politician, and judge. Noted for his *Sketches of New Brunswick* (1825). Elected to New Brunswick assembly in 1837. In 1854 he became first premier of New Brunswick following advent of responsible government and held that office for a second time 1857–1861. Appointed judge of Supreme Court of New Brunswick in 1868.

Peter Mitchell: Born January 4, 1824, in Newcastle, New Brunswick. Was a lawyer, businessman, author, and politician. Member of the New Brunswick House of Assembly and later the legislative council. A proponent of Confederation, he was premier of New Brunswick 1866–1867. Post-Confederation he was appointed to Senate of Canada and became Minister of Marine and Fisheries in the new federal government.

PRINCE EDWARD ISLAND

William Henry Pope
George Coles
John Hamilton Gray
Andrew Archibald Macdonald
Edward Palmer

Thomas Heath Haviland: Born November 13, 1822 at Charlottetown, Prince Edward Island. Lawyer, politician and militia officer. Elected to the Legislative Assembly of Prince Edward Island in 1846 and served until 1876. He became the third Lieutenant-Governor of the Island in 1879 and finished his career when he became Mayor of Charlottetown in 1886.

Edward Whelan: Born in 1824 in Ballina, County Mayo, Ireland. Was a journalist and orator. Spent early years in Halifax, Nova Scotia, where he worked as a printing apprentice to Joseph Howe. Elected to the Prince Edward Island Legislative Assembly in 1846. In 1851 he was named to the Executive Council and appointed Queen's Printer. He was an advocate of Confederation, which made him unpopular with the Islanders. He died in 1867.

NEWFOUNDLAND

Sir Frederick Carter: Born February 12, 1819. Was a lawyer and politician. He was premier of Newfoundland 1865–1870. He was a supporter of Confederation even though Newfoundland did not join Confederation until 1949. He was appointed Chief Justice of Newfoundland in 1880.

Sir Ambrose Shea: Born on or about May 15, 1815, in St. John's, Newfoundland. Was a newspaperman, politician, and governor of the Bahamas. He was elected to the Newfoundland House of Assembly in 1848 and again in 1855, when he was appointed Speaker. He was an advocate of Confederation and spoke enthusiastically in favour of the Quebec Resolutions. Newfoundlanders did not share his zeal. He was unsuccessful in his attempts to secure the governorship of Newfoundland and instead was given the post of governor of the Bahamas, which he held 1887–1894.

The London Conference, which produced the British North America Act leading to Confederation on July 1, 1867, was attended by sixteen delegates, thirteen of whom had attended either or both the Charlottetown and Quebec Conferences, in addition to three new Fathers of Confederation.

ONTARIO

Sir John A. Macdonald
William MacDougall

Sir William Pearce Howland: Born May 29, 1811, in Pawling, New York. Was a businessman and politician. Became a naturalized British subject in 1841. Became member of legislative assembly of Ontario in 1857. Held various positions in Cabinet. Post-Confederation became Member of Parliament and Minister of Inland Revenue until his appointment as Ontario's second lieutenant-governor in 1868.

QUEBEC

Sir George-Étienne Cartier
Sir Alexander Tilloch Galt
Sir Hector-Louis Langevin

NOVA SCOTIA

Sir Adams George Archibald
William Alexander Henry
Jonathan McCully
Sir Charles Tupper

John William Ritchie: Born March 26, 1808, at Annapolis Royal, Nova Scotia. Was a lawyer, legislator, and judge. Appointed to Nova Scotia Legislative Council as Solicitor General in 1864 and to the Canadian Senate in 1867. Was a judge of the Supreme Court of Nova Scotia 1873–1882.

NEW BRUNSWICK

John Mercer Johnston
Sir Samuel Leonard Tilley
Charles Fisher
Peter Mitchell

Robert Duncan Wilmot: Born October 16, 1809, in Fredericton, New Brunswick. Was a businessman and politician. Was a member of the New Brunswick Legislative Assembly 1847–1861 and 1865–1867. Post-Confederation he was appointed to the Canadian Senate where he became speaker in 1878. Upon resigning from the Senate, he served as the sixth lieutenant-governor of New Brunswick until 1885.

PRINCE EDWARD ISLAND

No attendees.

Appendix 2

Biography of Rear Admiral Hugh Francis Pullen, OBE

Hugh Francis Pullen was born at Oakville, Ontario, on July 9, 1905. He came from a family with a seagoing tradition that went back for more than a century and a half. This background spawned in him a keen interest in history and traditions of the naval service.

He was a grand nephew of Vice Admiral William John Samuel Pullen, who as a lieutenant on HMS *Plover* in 1848, took part in a failed search for Sir John Franklin. Franklin's expedition to discover the Northwest Passage in the Canadian Artic had ended in tragedy with the loss of both his ships, HMS *Erebus* and HMS *Terror*, and their crews. Vice Admiral Pullen made a second, also unsuccessful, search in 1852 as master of the HMS *North Star*. Years later, Rear Admiral H. F. Pullen and his younger brother, Captain Thomas C. Pullen, wrote about those separate expeditions to the Canadian Artic in "The Pullen Records."

H. F. Pullen attended Lakefield Preparatory College near Peterborough, Ontario, before entering the Royal Naval College at Esquimalt, British Columbia in 1920. After serving two years as a cadet with Canadian Pacific Steamship Company, Pullen returned to the RCN and went overseas for training with the Royal Navy. In 1925 he was posted to the British battleship *Hood*. Early in 1940 Pullen was given command of HMCS *Saint Francis* and spent time with the Clyde Escort Force in the hunt for the German battleship *Bismarck*.

He had a distinguished career in the RCN during times of both war and peace. He was awarded the Order of the British Empire for his services while commanding a convoy escort group in the Second World War. Following the war he was promoted to the rank of commodore in 1951, and rear admiral in 1953, a position he held until his retirement in 1960.

Rear Admiral Pullen retired to Chester Basin, Nova Scotia, from where he pursued his interest in research and writing. He was an accomplished

Rear Admiral Hugh Francis Pullen with Her Royal Highness Queen Elizabeth II in Halifax, Nova Scotia, 1959.

author of several books on maritime history and also held executive positions in many voluntary organizations. He was general manager of the Atlantic Pavilion at Expo 67 in Montreal. One of his most lasting contributions was as co-founder of the Maritime Museum of Canada, now the Maritime Museum of the Atlantic, in Halifax.

Rear Admiral Pullen was married to Helen (MacKean) and together they had seven children. He died on May 4, 1983, in England and was given a full military funeral in Halifax on May 10, 1983. He was awarded a posthumous Honourary Doctorate of Common Law from the University of King's College in Halifax.

Whether they know it or not, Canadians are indebted to Rear Admiral Hugh Pullen. Historians have inquiring minds and oftentimes a dogged determination to collect, compile, and disseminate information about some aspect of our history. Often they are not academic historians but people from varied backgrounds, all possessed with a common desire to preserve and perpetuate our history. Pullen was such a person, and but for his interest, perseverance, and letter-writing we may never have come to understand and appreciate how *Queen Victoria* and her bell have come to symbolize the efforts of our forefathers to create a united Canada.

Selected Bibliography

Books
Appleton, Thomas E. *Usque Ad Mare: a History of the Canadian Coast Guard and Marine Services.* Ottawa: Department of Transport, 1968.
Brown, Craig. *The Illustrated History of Canada.* Toronto: Lester & Orpen Dennys, 1987.
Bruce, Harry. *An Illustrated History of Nova Scotia.* Halifax: Nimbus Publishing and The Province of Nova Scotia, 1997.
Callbeck, Lorne C. *The Cradle of Confederation.* Fredericton: Brunswick Press, 1964.
Campbell, Duncan. *Nova Scotia in its Historical, Mercantile and Industrial Relations.* Montreal: John Lovell, 1873.
Dawson, R. MacGregor. *The Government of Canada,* 4th ed. Toronto: University of Toronto Press, 1963.
Graham, Gerald S. *A Concise History of Canada.* New York: Viking Press, 1968.
Gwyn, Richard. *John A The Man Who Made Us.* Vol. 1 (1815–1867). Toronto: Random House Canada, 2007.
Hennessey, Catherine G. David Keenlyside and Edward MacDonald, *The Landscapes of Confederation: Charlottetown, 1864.* Charlottetown: Prince Edward Island Museum and Heritage Foundation, 2010.
Hill, Kay. *Joe Howe: The Man Who Was Nova Scotia.* Toronto: McClelland and Stewart, 1980.
Jackman, W. J. *The Illustrious Life and Reign of King Edward VII.* Guelph, ON: World Publishing Company, 1910.
Kessler, Deirdre and Douglas Baldwin. *The Charlottetown Conference and the Birth of Confederation.* Halifax: Nimbus Publishing, 2015.
MacLennan, Hugh. *The Rivers of Canada.* New York: Charles Scribner's Sons, 1961.
Martin, Ged. *The Causes of Canadian Confederation.* Fredericton: Acadiensis Press, 1990.
Moore, Christopher. *Three Weeks in Quebec City.* London, UK: Allen Lane, 2015.
Napier, James. *Life of Robert Napier.* Edinburgh: William Blackwood and Sons, 1904.
Shortt, Adam and Arthur G. Doughty. *Canada and its Provinces.* Vol. 5. Toronto: Glasgow, Brook & Company, 1914.
Tulchinsky, Gerald J. J. *The River Barons.* Toronto: University of Toronto Press, 1977.
Waite, P. B. *The Life and Times of Confederation 1864–1867.* Toronto: University of Toronto Press, 1962.

Newspapers
Bangor Daily News, July 5, 2003; October 22, 2003; May 17, 2004; October 13, 2005; August 28, 2006; June 8, 2014; June 12, 2014; August 1, 2015; January 28, 2016; February 24, 2016.
British Colonist, September 20, 1856; September 13, 1864; September 13, 1864; September 18, 1866; October 30, 1866.

Colonial Standard, September 13, 1864; September 20, 1864; October 4, 1864; October 11, 1864; October 18, 1864; October 25, 1864.
Chicago Tribune, October 10, 1866.
Chronicle Herald, August 24, 1963; August 27, 1963; June 30, 2014.
Ellsworth American, December 14, 1966; April 10, 2015; July 18, 2016.
Examiner, September 5, 1864
Glasgow Herald, April 20, 1855; April 25, 1855; July 4, 1855: July 27, 1855; August 15, 1856.
Halifax Citizen, September 8, 1866; September 11, 1866; September 15, 1866; September 25, 1866; October 16, 1866; October 20, 1866; October 23, 1866.
Halifax Evening Reporter, September 10, 1864; September 15, 1864.
Halifax Morning Chronicle, August 19, 1864; September 1, 1864; September 4, 1866; September 11, 1866; September 18, 1866; September 19, 1866; September 20, 1866; September 24, 1866; September 25, 1866; September 27, 1866; September 28, 1866; October 3, 1866; October 10, 1866; October 12, 1866; October 19, 1866; October 22, 1866; October 25, 1866; October 26, 1866; November 8, 1866.
Halifax Morning Sun, August 17, 1864; August 22, 1864; September 12, 1866; September 28, 1866.
Halifax Sun & Advertiser, August 19, 1864; August 22, 1864; August 24, 1864; August 26, 1864; August 29, 1864; August 31, 1864; September 2, 1864; September 5, 1864; September 7, 1864; September 9, 1864; September 12, 1864; September 14, 1864: September 16, 1864; September 19, 1864; September 21, 1864; September 23, 1864; September 26, 1864; September 30, 1864; October 3, 1864; October 5, 1864; October 14, 1864; October 17, 1864; October 10, 1866; October 26, 1866.
Halifax Reporter, September 10, 1864.
Le Canadien, August 8, 1864; August 10, 1864; August 12, 1864.
Montreal Herald, August 9, 1864.
National Post, August 13, 2014.
New York Times, October 11, 1866.
Ottawa Citizen, November 24, 2014.
Quebec Gazette, February 14, 1805; August 22, 1811; August 30, 1856; September 3, 1856; September 9, 1856; September 12, 1856; September 16, 1856; September 18, 1856; September 22, 1856; September 23, 1856; September 26, 1856; September 29, 1856; October 1, 1856; October 7, 1856; October 11, 1856; October 14, 1856; October 18, 1856; October 24, 1856; October 25, 1856; June 12, 1857; July 10, 1857; September 25, 1857; November 11, 1857; November 16, 1857; November 18, 1857; April 30, 1858; May 26, 1858; May 28, 1858; May 31, 1858; June 2, 1858; June 14, 1858; June 18, 1858; August 30, 1858; December 1, 1858; June 27, 1859: July 1, 1859; August 12, 1859; October 3, 1859; July 6, 1866; July 9, 1866; July 12, 1866; August 8, 1866; August 24, 1866; August 27, 1866; August 29, 1866; August 31, 1866; September 5, 1866; September 14, 1866; September 21, 1866; September 24, 1866; October 10, 1866; October 15, 1866; October 19, 1866.
Quebec Mercury, August 4, 1864; August 5, 1864; August 6, 1864; August 10, 1864; August 25, 1864; August 27, 1864; October 20, 1890; October 22, 1890; October 23, 1890; November 5, 1890.
Saint John Telegraph, September 9, 1864.

Other

Annett, Ken. "Fathers of Confederation Visit Gaspé." n.d.
Annual Report (First) of Department of Marine and Fisheries (Canada), 1868; Annual Report (Third) of Department of Marine and Fisheries (Canada), 1870; Annual Report

(Fifth) of Department of Marine and Fisheries (Canada), 1872; Annual Report (Sixth) of the Department of Marine and Fisheries (Canada), 1873.

Congressional Record, March 25, 2014.

Gouldsboro Newsletter, April 2014; September 2016.

Gouldsboro Board of Selectmen's Meeting, Minutes, January 14, 2016.

Journal and Proceedings of the Nova Scotia House of Assembly, *Tallahassee*, Appendix 67, 1864.

Sessional Papers (Quebec) 23 Victoria, 1860; Sessional Papers (Quebec) 25 Victoria, 1862; Sessional Papers (Quebec) 26 Victoria, 1863; Sessional papers (Quebec) 29 Victoria 1865; Sessional Papers (Quebec) 30 Victoria, 1866; Sessional Papers (Quebec) 31 Victoria, 1867; Sessional Papers (Quebec) 38 Victoria, 1875.

Trinity House of Deptford Strond, *500 Years of the Corporation 1514–2014*, 2nd ed., 2014.

Trinity House, "2016 Fraternity Review."

Bibliography

Beck, J. Murray. "Joseph Howe Anti-Confederate," *The Canadian Historical Association*, Historical Booklet No. 17, Ottawa, 1965.

Beck, J. M. "Howe and the Enactment of the B.N.A. Act: Final Disillusionment of a Statesman of Empire," *Collections of the Nova Scotia Historical Society*. Vol. 40. Halifax, 1980.

Blakeley, Phyllis R. "Henry, William Alexander," in *Dictionary of Canadian Biography*. Vol. 11. University of Toronto/Université Laval, 2003–, www.biographi.ca/en/bio/henry_william_alexander_11E.html.

Bolger, Francis W. P. "The Charlottetown Conference and its Significance in Canadian History." CCHA, Report, 27 (1960): 11–23.

Bonenfant, J.-C. "Cartier, Sir George-Étienne," in *Dictionary of Canadian Biography*. Vol. 10. University of Toronto/Université Laval, 2003–, www.biographi.ca/en/bio/cartier_george_etienne_10E.html.

Brown, George. "Letter on the First Conference on Confederation at Charlottetown, P.E.I. September, 1864." Halifax, September 13, 1864.

Buckner, Phillip. "Tupper, Sir Charles," in *Dictionary of Canadian Biography*. Vol. 14. University of Toronto/Université Laval, 2003–, www.biographi.ca/en/bio/tupper_charles_14E.html.

Burns, Robin B. "McGee, Thomas D'Arcy," in *Dictionary of Canadian Biography*. Vol. 9. University of Toronto/Université Laval, 2003–, www.biographi.ca/en/bio/mcgee_thomas_d_arcy_9E.html.

Careless. J. M. S. "Brown, George," in *Dictionary of Canadian Biography*. Vol. 10. University of Toronto/Université Laval, 2003–, www.biographi.ca/en/bio/brown_george_10E.html.

"Charlottetown and Quebec Conferences of 1864," in *Dictionary of Canadian Biography*, University of Toronto/Université Laval, 2003–, www.biographi.ca/en/theme_conferences_1864.html.

Confederation Centre for the Arts. *The Iron Steamship* Queen Victoria. Charlottetown, n.d.

———. *The Bell of the S.S.* Queen Victoria. Charlottetown, n.d.

Corley, Nora. "The St. Lawrence Ship Channel 1805–1865." *Cahiers de geographie du Quebec*, vol. 11, no. 23 (1967).

Creighton, D. G. "The Confederation Conference."

Crummey, Michael. "The Circus Comes to Charlottetown, the Accidental Birth of a Nation." *The Walrus*, September 25, 2014.

Désilets, Andrée. "Chapais, Jean-Charles," in *Dictionary of Canadian Biography*. Vol. 11. University of Toronto/Université Laval, 2003–, www.biographi.ca/en/bio/chapais_jean_charles_11E.html.

———. "Langevin, Sir Hector-Louis," in *Dictionary of Canadian Biography*. Vol. 13. University of Toronto/Université Laval, 2003–, www.biographi.ca/en/bio/langevin_hector_louis_13E.html.

———. "Taché, Sir Étienne-Paschal," in *Dictionary of Canadian Biography*. Vol. 9. University of Toronto/Université Laval, 2003–, www.biographi.ca/en/bio/tache_etienne_paschal_9E.html.

Fleming, R. B. "Howland, Sir William Pearce," in *Dictionary of Canadian Biography*. Vol. 13. University of Toronto/Université Laval, 2003–, www.biographi.ca/en/bio/howland_william_pearce_13E.html.

Fraser, James A. and C. M. Wallace. "Johnson, John Mercer," in *Dictionary of Canadian Biography*. Vol. 9. University of Toronto/Université Laval, 2003–, www.biographi.ca/en/bio/johnson_john_mercer_9E.html.

Hiller, J. K. "Shea, Sir Ambrose," in *Dictionary of Canadian Biography*. Vol. 13. University of Toronto/Université Laval, 2003–, www.biographi.ca/en/bio/shea_ambrose_13E.html.

Jobb, Dean. "The Tale of the *Tallahassee*." National Post, August 13, 2014.

Johnson, J. K. and P. B. Waite. "Macdonald, Sir John Alexander," in *Dictionary of Canadian Biography*. Vol. 12. University of Toronto/Université Laval, 2003–, www.biographi.ca/en/bio/macdonald_john_alexander_12E.html.

Jones, Francis I. W. "A Hot Southern Town Confederate Sympathizers in Halifax During the American Civil War." *Journal of the Royal Nova Scotia Historical Society* vol. 2 (1999).

Kesteman, Jean-Pierre. "Galt, Sir Alexander Tilloch," in *Dictionary of Canadian Biography*. Vol. 12. University of Toronto/Université Laval, 2003–, www.biographi.ca/en/bio/galt_alexander_tilloch_12E.html.

King, Allan. "Halifax and the American Civil War." *Michigan Social Studies Journal*, vol. 14, no. 1 (Spring 2013).

Lévesque, Ulric. "Le Boutillier, John," in *Dictionary of Canadian Biography*. Vol. 10. University of Toronto/Université Laval, 2003–, www.biographi.ca/en/bio/le_boutillier_john_10E.html.

Macdonald, John A. Letter to Charles Tupper, September 20, 1864.

MacDonald, G. Edward. "Macdonald, Andrew Archibald," in *Dictionary of Canadian Biography*. Vol. 14, University of Toronto/Université Laval, 2003–, www.biographi.ca/en/bio/macdonald_andrew_archibald_14E.html.

MacKinnon, Neil J. "Ritchie, John William," in *Dictionary of Canadian Biography*. Vol. 11. University of Toronto/Université Laval, 2003–, www.biographi.ca/en/bio/ritchie_john_william_11E.html.

Marquis, Greg. "Mercenaries or Killer Angels? Nova Scotians in the American Civil War," *Collections of the Royal Nova Scotia Historical Society*, vol. 44, Halifax, 1996.

Monck, Frances E. O. "Leaves From My Journal In Canada, 1864–1865." London: Richard Bentley and Son, 1891.

Morgan, Henry J. *The Tour of His Royal Highness The Prince of Wales through British America and United States By a British Canadian* (Montreal: John Lovell, 1860).

Osborne, Brian D. "Robert Napier The Father of Clyde Shipbuilding." Dumbarton District Libraries, Dumbarton, Scotland, 1991.

Pryke, K. G. "Archibald, Sir Adams George," in *Dictionary of Canadian Biography*. Vol. 12. University of Toronto/Université Laval, 2003–, www.biographi.ca/en/bio/archibald_adams_george_12E.html.

Pullen, Rear Admiral H. F. "The S. S. *Queen Victoria* 1856–1866." Nova Scotia Archives and Records Management, UF, Vol 371, No. 10.

Pullen, Rear Admiral H. F. Correspondence Pullen-Noonan. Letter James E. Noonan to Pullen April 21, 1966; Letter Pullen to Noonan May 4, 1966. Queen Victoria File, Maritime Museum of the Atlantic, Halifax, Nova Scotia.

Pullen, Rear Admiral H. F. Correspondence Pullen-Ralph Allen. Letter May 19, 1966 Allen to Pullen; Letter Pullen to Allen June 3, 1966; Letter Allen to Pullen June 18, 1966; letter Pullen to Allen June 24, 1966. Queen Victoria File, Maritime Museum of the Atlantic, Halifax, Nova Scotia.

Robb, Andrew. "Haviland, Thomas Heath (1822–95)," in *Dictionary of Canadian Biography*.

Vol. 12. University of Toronto/Université Laval, 2003–, www.biographi.ca/en/bio/haviland_thomas_heath_1822_95_12E.html.

Robertson, Ian Ross. "Coles, George," in *Dictionary of Canadian Biography.* Vol. 10. University of Toronto/Université Laval, 2003–, www.biographi.ca/en/bio/coles_george_10E.html.

———. "Palmer, Edward," in *Dictionary of Canadian Biography.* Vol. 11. University of Toronto/Université Laval, 2003–, www.biographi.ca/en/bio/palmer_edward_11E.html.

———. "Pope, William Henry," in *Dictionary of Canadian Biography.* Vol. 10. University of Toronto/Université Laval, 2003–, www.biographi.ca/en/bio/pope_william_henry_10E.html.

Romney, Paul. "Mowat, Sir Oliver," in *Dictionary of Canadian Biography.* Vol. 13. University of Toronto/Université Laval, 2003–, www.biographi.ca/en/bio/mowat_oliver_13E.html.

Savard, Pierre and Paul Wyczynski. "Garneau, François-Xavier," in *Dictionary of Canadian Biography.* Vol. 9. University of Toronto/Université Laval, 2003–, www.biographi.ca/en/bio/garneau_François_xavier_9E.html.

Spray, W. A. "Mitchell, Peter," in *Dictionary of Canadian Biography.* Vol. 12. University of Toronto/Université Laval, 2003–, www.biographi.ca/en/bio/mitchell_peter_12E.html.

———. "Steeves, William Henry," in *Dictionary of Canadian Biography.* Vol. 10. University of Toronto/Université Laval, 2003–, www.biographi.ca/en/bio/steeves_william_henry_10E.html.

———. "Wilmot, Robert Duncan," in *Dictionary of Canadian Biography.* Vol. 12. University of Toronto/Université Laval, 2003–, www.biographi.ca/en/bio/wilmot_robert_duncan_12E.html.

Swainson, Donald. "Campbell, Sir Alexander," in *Dictionary of Canadian Biography.* Vol. 12. University of Toronto/Université Laval, 2003–, www.biographi.ca/en/bio/campbell_alexander_12E.html.

———. "Cockburn, James," in *Dictionary of Canadian Biography.* Vol. 11. University of Toronto/Université Laval, 2003–, www.biographi.ca/en/bio/cockburn_james_11E.html.

Swift, Michael. "Chandler, Edward Barron," in *Dictionary of Canadian Biography.* Vol. 10. University of Toronto/Université Laval, 2003–, www.biographi.ca/en/bio/chandler_edward_barron_10E.html.

Waite, P. B. "The Charlottetown Conference," *The Canadian Historical Association*, Historical Booklet, ,o. 15, Ottawa, 1963.

Waite, P. B., "McCully, Jonathan," in *Dictionary of Canadian Biography*, Vol. 10, University of Toronto/Université Laval, 2003–, www.biographi.ca/en/bio/mccully_jonathan_10E.html.

Wallace, C. M. "Gray, John Hamilton (1814–89)," (New Brunswick) in *Dictionary of Canadian Biography.* Vol. 11. University of Toronto/Université Laval, 2003–, www.biographi.ca/en/bio/gray_john_hamilton_1814_89_11E.html.

——— "Fisher, Charles," in *Dictionary of Canadian Biography.* Vol. 10. University of Toronto/Université Laval, 2003–, www.biographi.ca/en/bio/fisher_charles_10E.html.

———. "Tilley, Sir Samuel Leonard," in *Dictionary of Canadian Biography.* Vol. 12. University of Toronto/Université Laval, 2003–, www.biographi.ca/en/bio/tilley_samuel_leonard_12E.html.

Weale, David E., "Gray, John Hamilton," (Prince Edward Island) in *Dictionary of Canadian Biography*, Volume 11. University of Toronto/Université Laval, 2003–, www.biographi.ca/en/bio/gray_john_hamilton_1811_87_11E.html.

Werthman, Fred. "SS *Queen Victoria* and SS *Napoleon III* Historic and Technical Research and Application Report." Hull, Quebec: Canadian Museum of History, January 23, 2015.

Zeller, Suzanne. "McDougall, William," in *Dictionary of Canadian Biography.* Vol. 13. University of Toronto/Université Laval, 2003–, www.biographi.ca/en/bio/mcdougall_william_13E.html.

Image Credits

Alamy — 40
Author's collection — 12, 16, 19, 21, 72, 81, 102, 122, 124, 140, 149, 150, 156, 157, 158
Bridgeman Images — 23
Dictionary of Canadian Biography — 78
Ellsworth American — 132, 133, 147
Fred Werthman — 30
Greg A. Hartford — 120
Gouldsboro Historical Society — 138, 139
Illustrated London News — 64
iStock Photography — 11
Library and Archives Canada — 24, 28, 85, 103
Lighthouse Friends — 126
Maritime Museum of the Atlantic — 66, 176
McCord Museum — 38
Naval History and Heritage Command — 67
Parks Canada/Dusan Kadlec — 91
Public Archives and Records Office of the Government of PEI — 79, 86

Image Credits

Index

Numerals set in italics refer to images

A

Acadian Recorder, the 55, 167
Admiral 29, 31
Advance 29–30, 107
Age of Sail 119
Allen, Captain Rufus Henry 120–122, 130, 156
Almon, William Johnston 65, 69
Alward, David 150, 151
American Bell Association 140
American Civil War 52, 55, 63, 65, 71
American Revolution 83
Amherst, Jeffrey 83
Anticosti Island 12, 22, 124
Archibald, Adams George 60, 78, 167
Ariadne, HMS 39–40
Armour, Robert 18
Atlantic Advocate 132–133

B

Baby, Charles François Xavier 19–22, 26–*28*, 32–37
Baie-Comeau 12, 124
Bailey, Henry 121
Bay of Fundy 58, 99
Beaulieu, Domonique 46
Bedard, Zoël 125
Bell Collectors' Club of Ontario 140
Belledeau, Captain 74
Benjamin Wier & Company 69
Bossé, Joseph-Noel 37
Bowen, Roger 147–149, *150*, 153
British North America Act 104, 173
British North America (BNA) 8, 29, 37, 39, 41, 45, 51–53, 55–56, 61, 63, 73, 79, 88, 93, 101, 103, 109, 113, 166
Brown, George 76, 82, 84–85, 88, 89–90, 166
Buchanan, James 39
Buckley, Beatrice 147, 154
Burnet, David 17
Burns, George 26

C

Cabot, Sebastian 39
Cabot Strait 12
Calais 25
Campbell, Alexander 165
Canadian Coast Guard 103, 155
Canadian Museum for Human Rights 153
Canadian Museum of History 148, 151–154, 159
Canadian Pacific Steamship Company 131, 175
Canwest Global Communications 142, 153
Cap des Rosiers 20, 30, 33, 78
Caron, René-Édouard 37
Carter, Frederick 172
Cartier, George-Étienne 37–38, 41, 75, 87–88, 96, 166
Cartier, Jacques *11*, 13–14, 21, 73, 78
Chandler, Edward Barron 78, 168
Channel Islands 77
Chapais, Jean-Charles 170
Charles Robin & Company 77
Charlottetown Conference 57, 85, 97, 102, 104, 130, 140, 165, 173

Château de Versailles 25
Chesapeake Affair 64, 65
Chesapeake, USS 64
Clyde Escort Force 175
Cockburn, James 170
Coles, George 55, 80, 90, 169
Columbus, Christopher 84
Confederate Council of Trade in Canada 109
Confederation 18, 55, 61, 74, 101, 109, 131, 155, 173
Crane, Jonas 136–137, 146
Creighton, Donald 85
Crimean War 23, 24, 27
Crystal Palace Great Exhibition 26
Cunard Line 15, 25–26, 41, 117, 161
Cunard, Samuel 26, 118

D

Dacotah, USS 64, 65
Day, Robert 121
Dean, David 151
de Champlain, Samuel 13, 20, 51
Deep Sea Pilotage Authority 16
Department of Marine and Fisheries 18, 107
Department of Public Works 27
Dickey, Robert Barry 78, 81, 167
Dominion of Canada 18
Doris 21
Drinkwater, Charles 75
Dugua de Mons, Pierre 51
Dundas, George 56, 87
Duplessis, T. C. 110–112, 122

E

Edmonstone, William 18
Ella and Annie, USS 64
Ellsworth American 134
Empress Eugenie 23, 26
English Channel, the 25
Erebus, HMS 28, 175
Evening Star 113
Expo 67 136, 176

F

Fanning Bank 87
Fathers of Confederation 8, 77, *85*, 123, 132, 139, 141, 155, 165, 173
Fisher, Charles 171
Fisher, Richard 142, 143
Fleming, Sir Sandford 57
Flying Fish, HMS 39–40, 43
Fort Amherst 83
Fort Ramsay 77

G

Galt, Alexander Tilloch 41, 166
Gaspé 12, 20, 40–41, 53, 77, 104, 107
Gauvin, Nicolas 151
Ghiz, Joseph 142
Gibson, William 114
Glasgow Herald, the 24, 25
Globe and Mail, the 140
Gouldsboro Historical Society, the 154, 162
Gourdeau, Eugene 31, 123
Graham, Gerald S. 51
Grand Trunk Railway 99, 102
Gray, John Hamilton 55, 78, 80, 86, 89, 96, 168–169
Grosse Isle 29
Gulf of St. Lawrence 11–12, 16, 20, 45, 161
Guy, Hypolite 18

H

Halifax Chronicle, the 65
Halifax Citizen, the 68, 100, 108
Halifax Morning Chronicle, the 60, 67, 108
Halifax Morning Sun, the 59, 70, 71, 95
Haviland, Thomas Heath 172
Head, Anna Maria 32
Head, Edmund Walker 41–42, 45
Heather Belle 81
Henry, William Alexander 78, 167

Hero, HMS 39–40, 41–42
Holland, Samuel 73
Howe, Joseph 59–60, 104
Howland, William Pearce 173

I

Île d'Orléans 12, 128
Illustrated London News 25
Imperial Boards of Trade 18
Imperial Lights 20, 33, 78
Irby, Frederick Paul 18

J

John Le Boutillier & Company 77
Johnston, John Mercer 168

K

Kaenrath, Bryan 152
Keith, Alexander 65
King Francis I 11
King George III 83
King Henry VIII 14, 15

L

Lady Head 32, 33, 40, 41, 103, 107
Lambly, John 17, 124
Langevin, Hector-Louis 75, 94, 166
Le Boutillier, John 77, *78*
Lee, Clifford 143
Lee, W. H. 75
LeMesurier, H. 17
Lily, HMS 60, 104
Lincoln, Abraham 118
Lindsay, Errol B. 17
Lindsay, William 18
London Conference 173
Lord Provost 25–26
Lowe, Robert 32
Lozier, Jean-François 146, 150, 153

M

Macdonald, Andrew A. 80, 169
Macdonald, John A. 41, 87, 88, 94, 97, 99, 165

MacDonnell, Richard Graves 56
MacDougall, William 75
MacFadyen, Bill 144
MacLennan, Hugh 11, 53
Manly Muir, George 17
Maritime Museum of the Atlantic 176
Maritime Union 54–57, 59, 72, 80, 86–87, 90, 92
Mary Rose 15
Mason, James Murray 63
McCully, Jonathan 78, 92, 167
McDonnell, Richard Graves 99
McDougall, William 166
McGee, Thomas D'Arcy 57, 60, 75, 77, 166
McIver, David 26
McKay, David 30–31
McKernan, John Jr. 142
McKinney, Stephen N. 138
McNaught, Ian 7, 15, *16*, 161
Mitchell, Peter 171
Molson, John 14, 18, 19
Monck, Charles Stanley 45
Monck, Frances 46, 74
Montmagny, CGS 128
Montreal Trade Review, the 112
Morning Chronicle, the 71
Mowat, Oliver 170
Murray, Ian 135
Museum of Human Rights 154

N

Napier, James R. 29
Napier, Robert 26, 27, 28, 36, 117
Napoleon I 23, 124
Napoleon III (figure) *23*, 24, 26
Naughty Ladies Club 136–138, *139*, 141
Noonan, Harriett 135
Noonan, James E. 133, 134, 138, 157
Northumberland Strait 93

O

Ogilvy, John N. 18

O'Neill, Mark 148
Ottoman Empire 23

P

Page, John 21, 22
Palmer, Edward 80, 90, 169
Paris Exhibition 26
Pemberton, George 17, 37
Peninsula School 145, 153
Persia, RMS 25–29
Pictou, Nova Scotia 33, 40–41, 78, 93, 98–100, 103–104, 107–108, 112, 117
Pointe-des-Monts 12, 123, 124, *126*
Polynesia 35
Ponvert 116, 117, 118, 119, 120, 130, 156
Pope, William Henry 80, *81*, 85, 89, 169
Port of London 14–15
Port-Royal, Nova Scotia 13, 51
Pouliot, Paul 31, 45–47, 74, 83, 92, 112–113, 121, 125–127, 130, 155
Prince Albert 23–25, 39, 44
Prince Edward, Duke of Kent 23, 83
Prince of Wales (figure) 38–40, 42–46, 76–79
Prince of Wales (ship) 78, 81
Prince Philip, Duke of Edinburgh 15
Princess Anne, Princess Royal 15
Prospect Harbor, Maine 119, *120*, 131, 134–147, 157, 162
Prospect Harbor Women's Club 136–139, 141, 157
Pullen, Hugh Francis 131, 133–134, 157, 175–*176*

Q

Quebec Conference 100–104, 130, 173
Quebec Daily News, the 109
Quebec Gazette, the 18, 29, 31, 35, 107, 110, 111, 114, 122
Quebec Resolutions 104
Queen Elizabeth II (figure) 23, 139

Queen Elizabeth 2 (ship) 7, 15, 161
Queen Victoria (figure) 23, *24*, 25, 37–39, 44
Queen Victoria Bridge *38*
Quesnel, Jules 18

R

Rayside, William K. 17
Richelieu River 52
Ritchie, John William 173
River Clyde 25–26, 29–30, 36, 117
River Thames 14
Rivière-du-Loup 103
Robert Napier & Sons 25
Rodrigue, Pierre 17
Rose, John 41
Ross, John 41
Ross's Weekly 84, 92
Roussel, Antoine 18
Routh, H. L. 18
Royal Canadian Mounted Police 135
Royal Proclamation of 1763 12

S

Saguenay River 41, 42, 46, 47, 74
Sainte-Marguerite River 43
San Jacinto, USS 63, *64*
Sept-Îles 12, 124
Sewell, John 111
Shaw, Andrew 18
Shea, Ambrose 172
Simon, B. (alias LaFleur) 17
Slaymaker & Nichols' Olympic Circus 78–79, 90
Slidell, John 63
Spert, Sir Thomas 15
Stadacona (Quebec City) 13, *19*, 37, 51
Steeves, William Henry 78, 168
Stevenson, George 122
Stewart, John 17
St. John's, Newfoundland 39, 172

St. Lawrence River *11*–13, 16–22, 27, 29, 32, 35, 37, 41, 45, 52, 53, 76, 100, 103, 107, 109, 118, 123, 124, 155, 161
Strait of Belle Isle 12, 17, 20–21, 30
Symes, G. B. 17

T

Taché, Etienne Paschal 37, 171
Tahoma, USS 114
Tallahassee Affair 71
Tallahassee, CSS 65, *66*, 67–72, 83, 162
Talon, Jean 51
Taschereau, Jean-Thomas 37
Taylor, Zachary 66
Tehernaya 29
Tilley, Samuel Leonard 78, 86, 168
Toronto Leader, the 58
Trent, RMS 63, *64*
Trinity House of Montreal 18
Trinity House of Quebec 7, 17–18, 20, 33, 36, 42, 74, 76, 123–124, 127–128, 155
Trinity House UK 7, 15–17, 36, 161
Trois-Rivères 11
Trowell, Ian 139–141
Try, John 18
Tupper, Charles 57, 65, 69, 78, 85–86, 97–99, 167

U

UNESCO 13
United Empire Loyalists 52
University of King's College 176
University of Ottawa 162

V

Vassey, Brad 143
Victoria Bridge 38, 43

W

Waite, P. B. 89
War of 1812 64
Werthman, Fred 151
Whelan, Edward 99, 172
White House, the 39
Wilkes, Captain Charles 63
Wilmot, Robert Duncan 174
Wood, John Taylor 66–*67*, 68–70

Y

Young, Robert 17

Related Titles

Steam Lion: A Biography of Samuel Cunard

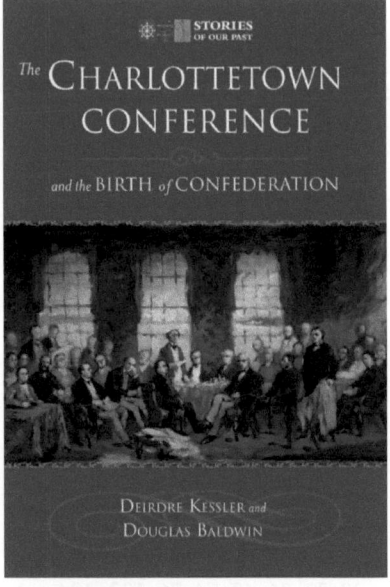

The Charlottetown Conference and the Birth of Confederation

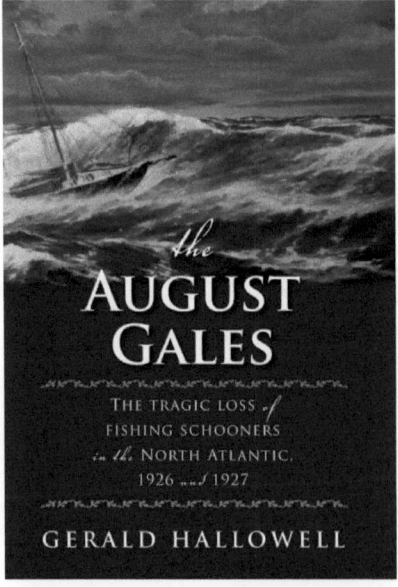

The August Gales: The Tragic Loss of Fishing Schooners in the North Atlantic

Printed by Libri Plureos GmbH in Hamburg, Germany